THE TRUTH ABOUT COLLEGE

RIC EDELMAN
#1 NEW YORK TIMES BESTSELLING AUTHOR

THE TRUTH ABOUT COLLEGE

THE ESSENTIAL GUIDE FOR
PARENTS AND TEENS
—SO YOU CAN MAKE THE RIGHT CHOICE
Together

WILEY

Copyright © 2026 by Ric Edelman. All rights reserved.

Published by John Wiley & Sons, Inc., Hoboken, New Jersey.

No part of this publication may be reproduced, stored in a retrieval system, or transmitted in any form or by any means, electronic, mechanical, photocopying, recording, scanning, or otherwise, except as permitted under Section 107 or 108 of the 1976 United States Copyright Act, without either the prior written permission of the Publisher, or authorization through payment of the appropriate per-copy fee to the Copyright Clearance Center, Inc., 222 Rosewood Drive, Danvers, MA 01923, (978) 750-8400, fax (978) 750-4470, or on the web at www.copyright.com. Requests to the Publisher for permission should be addressed to the Permissions Department, John Wiley & Sons, Inc., 111 River Street, Hoboken, NJ 07030, (201) 748-6011, fax (201) 748-6008, or online at http://www.wiley.com/go/permission.

The manufacturer's authorized representative according to the EU General Product Safety Regulation is Wiley-VCH GmbH, Boschstr. 12, 69469 Weinheim, Germany, e-mail: Product_Safety@wiley.com.

Trademarks: Wiley and the Wiley logo are trademarks or registered trademarks of John Wiley & Sons, Inc. and/or its affiliates in the United States and other countries and may not be used without written permission. All other trademarks are the property of their respective owners. John Wiley & Sons, Inc. is not associated with any product or vendor mentioned in this book.

Limit of Liability/Disclaimer of Warranty: While the publisher and the authors have used their best efforts in preparing this work, including a review of the content of the work, neither the publisher nor the authors make any representations or warranties with respect to the accuracy or completeness of the contents of this work and specifically disclaim all warranties, including without limitation any implied warranties of merchantability or fitness for a particular purpose. No warranty may be created or extended by sales representatives, written sales materials or promotional statements for this work. The fact that an organization, website, or product is referred to in this work as a citation and/or potential source of further information does not mean that the publisher and authors endorse the information or services the organization, website, or product may provide or recommendations it may make. This work is sold with the understanding that the publisher is not engaged in rendering professional services. The advice and strategies contained herein may not be suitable for your situation. You should consult with a specialist where appropriate. Further, readers should be aware that websites listed in this work may have changed or disappeared between when this work was written and when it is read. Neither the publisher nor authors shall be liable for any loss of profit or any other commercial damages, including but not limited to special, incidental, consequential, or other damages.

For general information on our other products and services or for technical support, please contact our Customer Care Department within the United States at (800) 762-2974, outside the United States at (317) 572-3993 or fax (317) 572-4002.

Wiley also publishes its books in a variety of electronic formats. Some content that appears in print may not be available in electronic formats. For more information about Wiley products, visit our web site at www.wiley.com.

Library of Congress Cataloging-in-Publication Data is Available:

ISBN 9781394406852 (Cloth)
ISBN 9781394406869 (ePub)
ISBN 9781394406876 (ePDF)

Cover Design: Wiley
Cover Image: © Lena/stock.adobe.com
Author Photo: Courtesy of the Author

SKY10128637_101525

To today's teenagers.
The world will soon be yours.

Contents

Preface
    Will College Set Your Teenagers on a Lifelong Path of Success,
    or Will It Ruin Their Life?   ix

Who Should Read This Book   xv

Chapter 1
    The Benefits of Getting a College Degree   1

Chapter 2
    The Perils of Going to College   15

Chapter 3
    People Loved College, Way Back When – These Days, Not So Much   21

Chapter 4
    So, Should College Be Your Goal?   25

Chapter 5
    If You Choose to Pursue a College Degree, Here's
    the Goal You Need to Set   35

CONTENTS

Chapter 6
In Truth, College Is Really About Lifestyle — 39

Chapter 7
The Cost of College — 55

Chapter 8
The Most Important College Choices You'll Make — 63

Chapter 9
How to Minimize the Cost of Getting a College Degree — 77

Chapter 10
The 12 Biggest Mistakes Students Make — 95

Epilogue
College Is Out – Lifelong Learning Is In — 177

20 Conversation Starters to Help Adults and Teenagers Talk About College — 181

Glossary — 189

Sources — 193

Acknowledgments — 223

Index — 227

Preface: Will College Set Your Teenagers on a Lifelong Path of Success, or Will It Ruin Their Life?

You are almost certainly encouraging the children in your life to go to college, and it's easy to see why. You know that those who hold college degrees generally have wealthier, healthier, longer and happier lives that are more enriching and impactful for themselves, their families and their communities than those who don't have college degrees.

But like any opportunity offering big benefits, there are costs and risks. That's why *your* behavior is crucial. Over the past 40 years, I've advised, trained, counseled and guided tens of thousands of parents, grandparents, step-parents and guardians, as well as countless teachers, high school guidance counselors, youth group mentors and other adults who are trying to positively influence youth. And when it comes to college planning, I've seen so many of these well-meaning folks make tragic mistakes that produce outcomes that are the opposite of what they wanted.

The Top 10 Mistakes

Here are the most common errors I've encountered throughout my career. Let's see how many of them you're guilty of:

1. Conveying through word, action and attitude that you expect your teenager to go to college. You oppose any suggestion from them that they might not want to go to college.
2. You have made it clear to your teenager that you expect them to pursue a particular career or to avoid certain careers.
3. In conversations with the teenager, you have cited others as role models, setting expectations that the teen must (or must not) follow the same college or career path.
4. Likewise, you have made it clear that there is a certain college or university (most commonly your alma mater, an Ivy League school, a military academy or a religious institution) that you expect them to attend.
5. Inversely, you have told them there are certain schools you do not want them to attend.

6. You have made it clear that you would be disappointed if they attended a community college.
7. You're the parent, grandparent, step-parent or guardian but haven't (yet) funded a college savings account in an amount sufficient to allow the teenager to graduate without any student debt.
8. You have told your teen that they must, or must not, live at home while they go to college.
9. You have told your teen that they must, or must not, work while school is in session.
10. You have conveyed to your teenager that they can attend any college or university of their choice. You have not placed any restrictions or parameters – such as cost or distance – on their decision as to which school to attend.

If you think few or none of these mistakes describe you, share the list with your teens and ask them if you've done any of them. If they feel they can safely be honest with you, the odds are pretty good that the ensuing conversation will be filled with significant revelations. This gives you an opportunity to change your behavior – before it causes the teenager to pursue a path that will lead to their ruin (and which could cause you the loss of tens or even hundreds of thousands of dollars).

Here's the key point: Rather than forcing (or merely "influencing") teenagers down a path of your own vision, you can help best by exposing them to the diverse opportunities that are available, guiding them toward selecting the path that is most likely to produce the best outcome for them.

PREFACE

This means you must not assume that all the teens in your life should go to college at all, let alone attend a specific school or pursue a specific degree. Simultaneously, you must not abdicate these choices solely to the child; no teenager has the experience or maturity to truly know if they should attend college (at all, let alone immediately after graduating high school), where to attend or what major to choose.

This is a big deal. If pursuing a college degree is the right path for each of the teens in your life, it is your responsibility to make certain that they manage their college experience correctly. If you succeed at this, they will enjoy the rewards.

But if you and they mismanage either the decision or the experience, that teenager could waste years of their lives; miss other, better career opportunities; and saddle themselves with massive amounts of debt that will haunt them for the rest of their life. Indeed, as you'll discover in these pages, college has destroyed the lives of millions of Americans, who as a result of their college experience have found it difficult to buy a car or home, or qualify for desired jobs, and many have avoided marriage or suffered divorce, become drug addicts or alcoholics or died by suicide.

Your teenagers will follow your lead. That means *you* must set the tone for them. This book will help you do that, so you both can navigate the college question effectively, and if you and they together decide they should pursue a college degree, they'll have a successful outcome.

For sure, reading this book will have a transformative, life-changing impact on the teenagers in your life.

What This Book Isn't

This book is not intended to be a damning analysis of our nation's higher education system. I'm not going to focus on what's wrong with our educational institutions or explain what policymakers in Congress and state legislatures should do about it.

I'm also not going to tell you how to save (or pay) for college. This is not a financial planning or investment advice book, so there's no discussion of 529 College Savings Plans or Tuition Pre-Payment Plans. No mention of converting those accounts to Roth IRAs, either.[1]

What This Book Is

Instead, this book has just one purpose: to give you and your teenagers the specific information you both need so that the student's post–high school experience helps them enjoy a long, rewarding and happy life.

And, above all, this book will help make sure that college doesn't ruin their life.

---
[1] Read my other books for that stuff.

Who Should Read This Book

You should read this book if you are a:

- Parent, grandparent, step-parent or guardian of a grade 7 to 12 student
- K–12 schoolteacher
- High school guidance counselor
- College admissions officer, professor, dean, provost or president
- Student in junior high or high school
- College student

The Unusual Convention I Used in Writing This Book

Although this book is vital for the previously cited adults, it's even more important for the students. Those in college-anticipation mode (meaning, starting in the seventh grade) need the information in this book to help them crystalize their plans. And it's not too late for students already in college to read this book (freshmen and sophomores will benefit more than juniors and seniors, obviously). Students need this information the most because, in the end, it's their life – and however they choose to proceed, they'll (be forced to) live with the consequences. The better prepared they are and the sooner they can prepare, the more likely they'll make decisions that are best for them.

Therefore, although the title and content (to this point) have been written from me to adults, I've written the rest of this book directly to the students. Adults will thus be eavesdropping on the conversation I'll be having with teens. And that's as it should be, because (as noted), it's the student who must live with the consequences (good and bad) of their college decisions. Besides, teens are more likely to listen to me than to the adults in their lives, because every teenager believes that every adult they know is an idiot.[1]

Even though I'll be talking to the students, don't take that to mean adults can skip the rest of the book. As I said, the biggest mistake adults make is abdicating the college decision to their high schoolers. So, you adults need to learn what your teens are about to learn – and that means reading this book along with (or prior to) them. This will allow you adults to decide how you feel about the information, strategies and advice contained herein – giving you the opportunity to have meaningful conversations with your teens, which will be life-changing for all of you.

---

[1] Recall Mark Twain's comment, "When I was a boy of 14, my father was so ignorant I could hardly stand to have the old man around. But when I got to be 21, I was astonished at how much the old man had learned in seven years."

And to help you engage in those conversations, you'll all find key takeaways at the end of each chapter, plus a helpful guide to talking with your teenagers at the end of the book.

But before you flip to the end, let's start at the beginning. In the first chapter, I'll explain to teens why they should seriously consider going to college.

Chapter One

The Benefits of Getting a College Degree

Ask any adult about the importance of going to college, and you're likely to get an answer that emphasizes career. Your parents, grandparents, step-parents or guardian, as well as high school guidance counselors and college admissions officers and recruiters, along with every well-meaning adult helping to set you on the path to prosperity and happiness, will tell you that a college degree lets you enter a career that offers more money than you'd otherwise be able to get.

They're not wrong.

And so, as we explore the many benefits of getting a college degree, that's where we'll start.

Better Salary

College graduates earn far more money than those who only have a high school diploma. And when I say "far more," I mean it: The Bureau of Labor Statistics says the average high school graduate earned $51,781 in 2024, while the average college graduate earned $120,302 – or 2.3 times more. Over an entire career, college grads earn a median $900,000 more than non-graduates, according to the Social Security Administration.

As you'll see in Chapter 6, college graduates are more likely to own their homes than those who only went to high school, and their homes are worth more, too. And the more a house is worth, the more it rises in value over time – helping college graduates retire with even greater wealth compared to those who never went beyond high school.

It's worth highlighting two factors that help explain why college graduates earn more money over their careers. First, they're more likely to be promoted than non-degreed workers (because they're more likely to be in careers that offer advancement), and promotions usually result in higher pay.

Second, college graduates are less likely to be out of work at any point; the unemployment rate, which rises and falls with economic conditions, is almost always nearly twice as high for those with only a high school diploma as it is for college graduates, according to the Pew Research Center.

Avoiding unemployment isn't just important for your future finances; it helps your mental health, too. Losing a job is extremely stressful, not least because you'll worry about paying your bills while you're unemployed. Half of workers who are laid off (known as *separated from service* because the employer eliminated many jobs, not just yours) take more than five months to find a new job, according to the Bureau of Labor Statistics.

And finding a job after losing one often forces people to relocate, which would disrupt your family and force you to incur moving-related expenses – resulting in even more stress. A 2019 Harris Poll found that more than half (53%) of those who only went to high school had been laid off at some point, compared to just 36% of college graduates. And when laid off, high school graduates were only about half as likely to be financially prepared as those with a college degree (43% versus 64%).

Thus, if you don't go to college, you're more likely to be stuck in the same low-paying job *and* more likely to lose it – and when you do, you'll be less likely to be financially prepared. Pretty strong arguments for getting a college degree.

Consider all this if you aren't yet persuaded that a college degree is a great path to financial success. And while you're at it, also consider this: The higher income you'll get thanks to your degree will give you a better opportunity to save and invest (thus providing the ability to build wealth) compared to people with lower incomes.

How Salary Leads to Wealth

That last point is important, because there are only three ways people get money in America: earn it, inherit or marry into it, or win it (through gambling and lotteries). The odds of success via gambling and lotteries are astronomically small, so we'll set that aside. And if you're like most Americans, any inheritance you get will be so small or so far into the future that it isn't worth discussing here. Equally unlikely is the notion that you will "marry up" – meaning securing a spouse who's wealthy. So, we'll also put aside inheritances and marrying someone rich.

That leaves you with only one avenue: you'll have to earn whatever money you hope to have in the future. That's actually the official name: The Internal Revenue Service calls it *earned income*. Yet, it's barely enough for most people to pay their basic costs of living: housing, utilities, food, clothes, transportation, health care and insurance.

After paying those bills, most Americans have no money left for entertainment, dining out or vacations. I'm not saying no one ever goes out for dinner (they sure do!). But since they've spent all their income on necessities, they must use credit cards for everything else – and that's a disastrous behavior. You see, if you use a credit card to pay a $25 restaurant tab, you'll not only have to repay that "principal" (the amount you borrowed), you'll also have to pay interest to the credit card company to compensate them for paying that tab when you weren't able to. Every dollar you pay to credit cards for luxuries (and frivolities) is a dollar you can't use to pay your basic expenses. And the less money you have to buy necessities, the more you'll use credit cards. This downward spiral lands millions of people in dire financial circumstances. Indeed, Americans in 2025 owed $1.2 trillion in credit card debt, an average of $6,000 per U.S. household, according to the Federal Reserve Bank of New York.

Here's why using credit cards is the path to poverty: If you make purchases totaling $10,000 in cash, you spend $10,000. But if you use credit cards for those purchases and then pay the minimum monthly payment ($225), you won't pay off the cards for five years, according to Experian, and you'll end up repaying $16,036. That's because the average credit card user pays 21% in annual interest charges.

But some people – mostly college graduates – earn lots of money. Not only can they pay their monthly bills in full, they can also pay for luxuries like eating out and taking vacations without going into credit card debt. Even after they splurge, they *still* have money left over, which they can put into savings and investments. Thus, instead of *paying* interest, they get to *earn* interest – and this is the magic formula that allows people in America to amass wealth.

This is the big secret that no one in the American education system tells you about. You're led to believe that you need a good education so you can get a good job and earn a good salary. That's true, but it's not the full story. You see, it's not enough that you earn a good salary. Your salary must be *so* good that you are able to put some of it into savings and investments.

You see, a high earned income lets you enjoy a nicer lifestyle than is possible with a lower income. But lifestyles are fleeting; they depend on income that's only as secure as the job that provides it. One day, you won't have that job. You'll quit, get fired or laid off, become disabled from illness or injury, or retire. Inevitably, therefore, your job will cease, and when it does, your income ceases, too.

That's why you need more than earned income. You need *wealth*. Because with wealth, you can maintain your lifestyle even when your earned income ceases or is interrupted.

And the only way you can reliably accumulate wealth is to put some of your earned income into savings and investments. But you can do that only if your income is high enough to pay your bills and splurge on luxuries – and still have money left over.

So, you should want a high income – and you're far more likely to get a job that pays a high income if you have a college degree than if you don't have one.

Better Benefits (Almost Like "Free Money")

A higher salary is just the first of the financial benefits of a college degree. Better-paying jobs also tend to offer more and better benefits, including:

- **Paid vacation:** You'll likely get paid even when you're on a two-week vacation (for someone earning a $75,000 annual salary, that's worth nearly $3,000 a year).
- **Paid sick leave:** You'll probably also get two to four weeks of paid time off when you're sick (or caring for a sick family member). That's worth another $3,000 to $6,000 yearly.
- **Paid health insurance:** Your employer will also probably pay for some or all the cost of health insurance for you, your spouse and your children. Paying for this yourself would cost you more than $25,000 a year for a family of four, according to KFF, a health policy research firm.
- **Paid child care:** Good jobs also often come with free child-care services. Otherwise, you'll spend an average of $16,000 per year per toddler, according to Care.com.
- **Free money added to your retirement savings:** Just about every midsize and large employer puts money into a retirement

savings account for their employees. The average employer-paid contribution is 4.6% of your salary, or $3,450 per year (again, assuming a $75,000 salary), according to Vanguard.

Some employers also provide free breakfast and lunch, eyeglasses, dental care, pet-care services, laundry and dry-cleaning services, health club memberships, transportation and parking subsidies, tuition reimbursement (so you can get a bachelor's or master's degree for free, which I'll cover in more detail later) and other benefits.

And all these benefits are tax-free! If you had to pay for them yourself, you'd have to pay taxes on their value, and that means, for example, you'd not only pay $16,000 for child care, you'd pay another $4,800 in taxes (assuming a combined 30% federal and state income tax bracket).

The bottom line: For those with high-paying jobs, 50% of your total compensation is in the form of benefits, according to Benepass. (So, when applying for a job, don't just ask, "What is the salary?" Instead, ask, "What is the total compensation? Please tell me about the benefits.")

For sure, those with a college degree are far better off financially than those without one. In fact, one in eight people who only have a high school diploma are living in poverty, according to Statista. That's three times more than those who have a college degree.

Better Work-Life Balance

All this talk about careers and money might be boring (or even annoying) you. After all, you know there's so much more to life than work.

You're right. But forgive me for putting career and money first, because older folks like me (Baby Boomers and Gen Xers) tend to believe that career achievement and financial prosperity are the measurements of success. I mean, not only didn't we attempt to achieve a "work-life balance," we'd never even heard of the phrase.

But you get it, and so do the adults in your life. And I'll happily concede the point: You're right. There is indeed so much more to life than work, and those who fail to live by this dictum eventually lament their choices with great regret.

But before the elders eavesdropping on this conversation admonish you to toss this book into the trash, let me make one very important point: Yes, there's more to life than work. But if you're a high school or college student, the life you hope to enjoy will be largely dictated by the amount of money you earn – and that means we can't ignore the importance of a great education. And college can deliver it all to you: a wonderful occupation that delivers tremendous job satisfaction and high income, plus an equally desirable and fulfilling lifestyle outside of work.

Indeed, 10 of the top 13 jobs where people report the highest levels of satisfaction with work-life balance require an associates, bachelor's, master's or doctoral degree: actuaries, clergy, data scientists, dental hygienists, dietitians and nutritionists, environmental engineers, epidemiologists, occupational therapists, optometrists and (yay!) personal financial advisors. Only 3 of the top 13 don't need a degree (recreation and fitness workers, landscapers/groundskeepers and musicians/singers). The data, compiled by Forage based on research from *U.S. News,* Payscale, the Bureau of Labor Statistics, MyPerfectResume and The Conference Board, suggest that you are far more likely to enjoy a great work-life balance if you have a college degree than if you don't.

Better Health

Now we're really getting to the fun stuff. More money and better benefits are just the start of how having a college degree is so advantageous for you. By having a degree, you'll also be healthier and live longer!

It's true. Degree holders are better informed about health and have employer-paid insurance, allowing them to visit the doctor more frequently at minimal cost. As a result, they are more likely to get and follow medical advice and engage in preventive care and healthy lifestyles, reducing the likelihood that they'll get sick. Only 5% of college graduates smoke, for example, compared to 17% of those with only a high school diploma, according to the Centers for Disease Control.

College grads also know more than non-grads about the importance of a nutritious diet – and thanks to their higher incomes, they can afford higher-quality food. College graduates also exercise more regularly than non-grads and can more easily afford to join a gym or health club.

And when college graduates do fall ill or get injured, they seek medical help faster than people who don't have insurance – because they're not as worried about the cost and because they know their employers tend to be tolerant when you miss work due to doctor visits. This helps them cure what's ailing them faster, with fewer complications and less likelihood that their health will deteriorate. And thanks to their paid sick leave, they can stay home and care for themselves, secure in the knowledge that they won't suffer any loss of income. People without that benefit must go to work – increasing the risk that they'll become even sicker than they already are – and possibly infecting co-workers.

College graduates are also more likely to have jobs with stable schedules – no overtime or shift work – and this helps them enjoy more and better sleep.[1] Their superior financial status compared to those without degrees translates into fewer incidents of stress, which dozens of studies have shown damages your health over time. (For example, when you're earning six figures, you are more able to afford a housekeeper to clean your home, so you can devote that time to family, friends and fitness.) All this means that college graduates are less likely to develop heart disease, diabetes, high blood pressure, depression and mental health disorders compared to those with less education, according to the Office of Disease Prevention and Health Promotion at the U.S. Department of Health and Human Services.

Add it all up, and you'll discover that individuals with a bachelor's degree, on average, live about seven years longer than those who only graduated from high school, according to a 2024 study by the Institute for Health Metrics and Evaluation at the University of Washington's School of Medicine.

Better Relationships

Your marriage is also likely to last longer if you have a college degree. The Bureau of Labor Statistics found that, of those who married, 27% of college graduates have gotten divorced, compared to 50% of those

---

[1] There are exceptions to this, of course. For example, hospital nurses work in shifts.

with only a high school diploma. That's no surprise, since 54% believe a partner with debt is sufficient reason to divorce, according to a SunTrust survey.

College-educated individuals tend to marry later in life, suggesting that by the time they marry, they are more mature, have more financial stability and select more compatible mates (college graduates tend to seek partners with similar aspirations) – all factors contributing to better, stronger and longer-lasting marriages.

Getting a college degree also helps you build a better foundation for the children you may have. Since you'll be able to live in a nicer, safer neighborhood, your children will get to attend better schools. They'll be more likely to participate in youth programs that boost their development. And children of parents who have a college degree are more likely to get a college degree than children of parents who didn't go to college. Indeed, 7 in 10 children of college-educated parents go to college themselves. That's nearly three times more than children whose parents didn't go to college, according to the Pew Research Center. Children of college graduates are also more likely to have higher household incomes in adulthood, following in the footsteps of their parents. They are also more likely to have better health behaviors and access to health care.

The benefits don't merely flow downline; they rise upline and travel sideways, too. College graduates tend to have stronger relationships with their parents and siblings than those who don't go to college, according to the National Institutes of Health. College graduates also have more and better friendships – not just with someone to have a beer or coffee with, but people they can rely on for support, from a shoulder to cry on to a place to stay in a crisis. The American Survey Center says Americans with a college degree are 50% more likely than non-grads to have a "third place" to hang out – a social setting like a park, coffee shop or bar. Having a third place is associated with positive social outcomes, including feeling more connected to one's community and experiencing less loneliness. Indeed, relationships forged in college can last a lifetime, further helping you enjoy social happiness (as well as greater access to professional opportunities you otherwise wouldn't have).

Better Community Engagement

Thanks to their education, college graduates also have better analytical and decision-making abilities, which are very helpful in everyday life and highly valued in the workforce, according to Northeastern University. Grads also rightly view their degree as a significant accomplishment, and this boosts their confidence and self-worth.

Small wonder, then, that college graduates are more likely to engage in society. They are more than twice as likely to vote, volunteer and participate in community activities as those without a bachelor's degree, and they contribute nearly 3.5 times more money to charity, according to the Association of Public and Land-Grant Universities.

Better, Better, Better

Work-life balance. Higher salaries. Superior benefits. Better health. Longer lifespans. Stronger marriages. Better outcomes for children.

Improved relationships with parents and siblings. More friends. Superior community involvement.

Such massive benefits of getting a college degree! Why would anyone hesitate to go to college?!? Perhaps it's because there are real dangers in doing so. We'll talk about them next.

 Key Takeaways

1. There are lots of benefits of getting a college degree, including:
   - **(a)** Better salary
   - **(b)** Better benefits
   - **(c)** Better work-life balance
   - **(d)** Better health
   - **(e)** Better relationships
   - **(f)** Better community engagement
2. Earning high income doesn't necessarily lead to wealth. Many people "spend up to their incomes" – meaning their lifestyles improve as their incomes rise. It might be fun to use a pay raise to buy a nicer car, but that leaves you just as poor as you were. Thus, it's vital that you place some of your income into savings and investments. That's the most reliable way to build wealth over time – and the higher your income, the more you'll be able to save. Since college graduates tend to earn higher incomes than those who don't have a degree, college grads are more likely to become wealthy than non-grads.

Chapter Two

The Perils of Going to College

Having read the prior chapter, *golly, getting a college degree sure sounds great!*

Only, that's not what most college graduates say. More than half (51%) of those polled by Strada Education and Gallup said they chose the wrong school or major. And a quarter of college graduates told *USA Today* that they wish they'd skipped college altogether.

Why do so many express such regret? There are lots of reasons, so let's look at each of them.

Mismatch Between College Major and Future Career

More than 40% of college graduates in their twenties work in jobs outside their field. Even worse, many of their jobs don't even require a college degree, according to the Pew Research Center. And the Strada Education Foundation and Burning Glass Institute found that, 10 years after graduating, barely half of graduates (55%) are working in jobs that require any degree, let alone the one they have.

If only half are happily working in their field after graduation, is a successful college outcome really nothing more assured than a coin toss?

Think about this before you decide to spend maybe a quarter of a million dollars and six years of your life on an endeavor that has a one-in-two chance of failure.

Saddled with Student Loans and Huge Opportunity Costs

Even if you do get a great job in your field, you might not be better off. The Federal Reserve Bank of St. Louis looked at the wealth of U.S. households and found that college graduates do have higher incomes than those who didn't graduate, but they don't accumulate more wealth. That's because most grads use a large portion of their higher incomes to pay off their student loans – debts that people who didn't go to college didn't accumulate and thus don't have to repay. Perhaps this helps explain why Aspen Economic Strategy Group found in 2024 that nearly 9% of those ages 30 to 40 still live with their parents; they aren't earning enough to live independently.

And graduates spent, on average, six years getting their degrees, meaning those who didn't go to college had six additional years of income. That group was able to compound their savings for six extra years, compared to college graduates. So even though the college graduates earned more money than those who didn't go to college, those higher earnings didn't translate into more wealth for them.

In other words, lots of people would be better off getting a lower-paying job at age 18 than a higher paying job at age 24. Might you be one of them?

Attending vs. Graduating

And all that assumes you graduate. But 37 million college students never did. Yup, 16% of U.S adults entered college but left without a degree, according to the National Student Clearinghouse Research Center. A quarter (24%) of freshmen drop out, and only 62% graduate after six years. Even though none of these people are getting the benefits of a degree, they're saddled with the lost years of missed income while they were in college, plus all the student debt they'd accumulated while in college.

Mental Health and Trauma

Are you finding this depressing? You're not alone. The cost, time and uncertain outcome of college is so daunting that depression is in fact rampant among college students. The National Alliance on Mental Illness says half (49%) of college students have been diagnosed with or treated for depression, with 20% of students in "serious psychological distress." The U.S. Department of Education and the American College Health Association's 2024 National College Health Assessment found that among those with student loans, the depression rate is 79%. These surveys have found that 50% of students are stressed, 49% suffer from loneliness, 48% are anxious and 44% feel hopeless.

Why are virtually half of all college students feeling so despondent? Their survey answers explain it all:

- Nearly six in 10 college students (57%) have been bullied.
- More than half (54%) have been sexually harassed.
- More than half (53%) have been cyberbullied.
- Half (49%) have experienced discrimination.
- Half (49%) have been hazed.
- More than a third (37%) have been victims of microaggressions.
- Nearly one in three (31%) has been sexually assaulted.
- More than one in four (27%) has been physically assaulted.

It gets worse. As a result of their experiences, 10% of undergrads have intentionally cut, burned, bruised or otherwise injured themselves, and 2% have tried to commit suicide. And that's just in the 2024–2025 school year. The Student Loan Planner's 2024 Mental

Health Survey of college students found that, of undergrads with student loans, 6% have had suicidal thoughts at some point. Nationwide, more than 24,000 college students attempt suicide every year, and 1,100 of them die. Two-thirds (65%) of college students know a classmate who attempted or died from suicide.

In the 18–25 age group, which represents the bulk of the college student population, 7.5% have seriously considered suicide in the past year, nearly double the 4% rate among the overall adult population, according to the American Foundation of Suicide Prevention. Furthermore, 3% of 18- to 25-year-olds made a plan to die by suicide, and 2% made an attempt.

From Chapter 1, it's clear that college degrees offer the opportunity for a happy life. But this chapter shows that happiness has eluded a great many people. So, should you go to college or not? You'll discover what people say in the next chapter.

 **Key Takeaways**

1. A quarter of college graduates wish they'd never gone to college. The reasons they cite:
   (a) The major they selected didn't match their eventual career.
   (b) Going to college forced them to amass large amounts of student loans that are adversely impacting their lives.

(Continued)

(*Continued*)
- **(c)** They paid a lot in *opportunity costs* – meaning the decision to go to college and amass their debt prevented them from pursuing other paths that may have provided better outcomes.
- **(d)** Most attended but never graduated – yet they still have the debt they incurred, and the years they spent at college were years of lost income (one of the opportunity costs).
- **(e)** Large numbers of students suffered mental health issues (including depression and thoughts of suicide) and other traumas.

Chapter Three

People Loved College, Way Back When – These Days, Not So Much

Society's views of the value and importance of a college education have shifted significantly over the past decade.

In 2015, 57% of Americans said college was a "great deal." By 2023, this figure had dropped to 36%, according to Gallup polls. The Pew Research Center found that half the country (49%) says having a college degree is less important than it was 20 years ago, while a Go1 survey showed that 46% of workers feel college didn't teach them the skills they need for their jobs. Nearly as many business leaders (40%) agreed, saying in an Intelligent.com survey that college graduates are ill-prepared to enter the workforce.

This helps explain why only 54% of parents in a 2021 Carnegie survey said they wanted their children to enroll in college immediately after high school – even if they could easily afford the cost. And most can't; in a 2024 survey by enrollment-management consulting firm EAB, 60% of parents said cost is their number-one concern about sending their kids to college. High school seniors are equally concerned about the cost of college: 59% said it's too expensive and not worth the cost, according to a 2022 survey by the Gates Foundation.

In these and other surveys, both high school seniors and parents also expressed:

- fear that substantial student loan debt would outweigh the benefits of obtaining a degree;
- uncertainty about their or their child's career path;
- concern that college might harm their or their child's mental health; and
- awareness that there are plenty of good jobs that don't require a college degree.

No wonder the proportion of high school students applying to college declined from 71% in 2015 to 61% by 2023, according to the National Center for Education Statistics. That's a decline of nearly 15%.

It used to be said that going to college right after high school was axiomatic. Nowadays, that's no longer true.

Key Takeaway

1. Only a third of Americans say college is a "great deal." This means you have to be deliberate and assertive so your college experience is, in fact, great.

Chapter Four

So, Should College Be Your Goal?

"I want to go to college."

I've heard that comment so many times that I've lost count. And it's a terrible thing for anyone to say!

It's terrible because it's merely a process statement, not a goal. Those who focus on process often fail, because the time, effort, cost, sacrifices or demands can be more challenging than they anticipated. But by focusing on the goal, you are more able to mentally focus on the mission, and that means less attention on the challenges you meet along the way.

This is not mere wordsmithing; I'm talking about an essential element of achievement. That's why the phrase "go to college" is a dangerous, distracting focus on process. Instead, frame the goal correctly: "get a college degree."

Think about it: If your goal is merely to "go to college," well, gee, you've accomplished that goal the day you arrive on campus as a freshman. But getting a degree requires that you complete your education – which takes far more time, effort and cost.

If you want to succeed in life, you must have goals and you must set them carefully. Otherwise, you won't achieve success. You must define what success means to you, and everyone does so differently. Some people want wealth; others want children; still others want to solve a social problem. Goals don't have to be mutually exclusive, by the way. You can have many goals – including the three that I just mentioned (and many more)!

My point is that you must start with a goal. It must be specific, definitive and impactful – and it must have a deadline. "I want to go to college" doesn't qualify. Neither does "I want to get a college degree." But this does: "I want to get a college degree in four years." See the difference?

But even that sentence isn't enough. *Why* do you want to get a degree in four years?

Think about that question for a moment before continuing.

. . .

If you're setting goals properly, you'll realize "getting a degree in four years" isn't the best possible goal. That's because the degree itself is also merely a process. What you really want – your *true* goal – is to acquire the knowledge and skills you need to be able to work or serve in a given field. *That's* the goal you want to establish and focus on.

Most people who go to college ignore or are oblivious to this notion. They assume that a college degree is all they need to enter and work in their preferred field. But that assumption is often false.

So, let's start with proper goal setting. And we'll start at the beginning with the question that adults have been asking you since you were a small child:

"What do you want to be when you grow up?"

The problem with this question is that it suggests you ought to know the answer. Seriously? You were asked this when you were as young as five years old! Even most 16-year-olds can't answer this! Good for you if you can, but don't feel bad if you aren't sure how to reply.

Indeed, the vast majority of high school students have no idea what career they want to pursue, demonstrated by the fact that 75% of college freshmen, according to Central College, are *undecided* or *undeclared* when they enter college (meaning they haven't selected a major field of study yet), and 80% of all college students change their majors at least once, according to the Student Research Group.

If you're among this large majority of college students, you can't be sure that college is the best choice. That's because there are hundreds of fulfilling, financially rewarding and emotionally enriching careers that don't require that you have a college degree.

As mentioned earlier, the average U.S. worker who holds a college degree earns $102,000 a year. But you don't need a degree to get that salary. None of the high-paying jobs listed in Table 4.1 require a college degree.

There are hundreds of more high-paying occupations; some of them require nothing but experience. You can prep for others by

Table 4.1 High-Paying Jobs That Don't Require a College Degree

Occupation	Average Salary
Commercial Pilots	$99,600
Police Detectives and Supervisors	$99,300
Nuclear Technicians	$99,300
Power Distributors and Dispatchers	$98,500
Transportation, Storage, and Distribution Managers	$98,200
Elevator and Escalator Installers and Repairers	$97,900
Radiation Therapists	$82,800
Ship Engineer	$82,400
Subway and Streetcar Operators	$81,200
Dental Hygienists	$77,800

Source: Adapted from The Armed Services Vocational Aptitude Battery.

getting a certificate from a vocational or technical school. In other words, yes, you must continue your education after you graduate from high school. But no, it doesn't necessarily mean you must pursue a college degree.

So, let's figure out if college is the right path for you. Answer the following questions.

1. What interests you? What do you enjoy doing?

Just about everything you like to do, you can engage in as a career. Just one example: Many colleges and universities now offer full scholarships to video gamers, same as football players. Esports is a $2 billion industry globally and projected to grow to $9 billion by 2032. The top 200 gamers each earn $1 million or more by competing in tournaments – events that are so popular that nearly seven million people watched the League of Legends 2024 World Championship.

All this explains why the Ric Edelman College of Communication, Humanities & Social Sciences at Rowan University (yep, named after me) lets students earn an online Esports Industry & Entertainment Experience certificate.

If there are such career opportunities in video gaming, imagine what's available in your own area of interest!

2. What concerns you?

You're old enough to know that life isn't perfect. A great many challenges confront us all every day. Consider this (unfortunately long) list:

- Addiction
- Ageism
- Animal Rights
- Arms Control
- Bullying
- Censorship
- Child Labor
- Chronic Disease
- Civil Liberties
- Climate Change
- Conservation
- Consumer Protection
- Corruption
- Crime
- Criminal Justice Reform
- Disability Rights
- Education Access
- Epidemics and Pandemics
- Ethics
- Extinctions
- Food Deserts
- Food Security
- Foreign Aid

- Fraud
- Freedom of Speech
- Geopolitical Conflicts
- Globalization and Trade
- Gun Violence
- Health Care Disparities
- Homelessness
- Housing Affordability
- Human Rights
- Hunger
- Immigration
- Indigenous Rights
- LGBT+ Rights
- Living Conditions
- Malnutrition
- Mental Health
- Natural Disasters
- Nuclear Weapons
- Ocean Dumping
- Overfishing
- Parental Rights
- Political Instability
- Pollution
- Poverty
- Prisoners' Rights
- Privacy and Surveillance
- Public Health
- Public Safety
- Quality of Life
- Racial Justice
- Racism
- Reproductive Rights
- School Choice
- Scientific Ethics
- Sexism
- Social Inequality
- Substance Abuse
- Terrorism
- Toxic Waste
- Urban Development
- Urban Planning
- Voter Suppression
- War and Conflict
- Women's Rights
- Worker's Rights

I suspect you don't know what some of these terms mean – and that's a great opportunity for you to go learn about them. One might become your life's calling!

3. What *haven't* you considered?

It's difficult to reply to a negative, so here's my point: It's a big world out there, and you've seen only a very small part of it so far. That's one of the top benefits of college: the classes you take, the activities you engage in, and the people you meet, all introduce you to the world and everything it offers. That's why so many college students change their majors: They discover something new and get so excited about it that they decide to make it their career choice.

The best news is that you don't have to attend college to make these discoveries. Hundreds of websites, thousands of books and countless mentors (family elders, community leaders and your teachers) are happy to suggest fields that are unknown to you – as are ChatGPT and other AI platforms. The content is growing so quickly that any list I'd offer you here would quickly become out-of-date, so the best approach is for you to simply explore the aforementioned and see what resonates.

Don't be surprised if you are (or become) interested in more than one subject. Well-rounded people always are! This means either you'll choose one as your primary occupation, with everything else being an avocation (hobby or volunteer activity) or you'll engage simultaneously in two or more of these subjects, juggling the commitments of time and attention that each takes. And this may shift over time as your interests and opportunities evolve. There's no right or wrong – just decide what feels right for you.

The key word there is *you*. Your career path is yours, not your father's and not your mother's. Too often, adults try to dictate to the teenagers in their lives what careers those teens ought to pursue, and that can lead to unhappiness for everyone. This is your life and no one else's. If what you're doing is honest, ethical, economically self-sufficient (meaning you can live comfortably without going into debt or relying on family and friends for financial support) and personally rewarding, then no one has a right to argue with your decisions.

So, when someone asks what you want to be when you grow up, give the one answer they won't be able to argue with.

"I want to be happy."

 Key Takeaways

1. Set the right goal, and use specific language that clearly articulates the outcome you seek. For example, "I want to go to college" is not as precise or helpful as "I want to get a college degree in four years."
2. If you're among those who are undecided about what major to choose, you can't be sure that college is the best choice for you right now. There are hundreds of financially rewarding and emotionally enriching careers that don't require you to obtain a college degree.

3. To help you determine if college is the right path for you, answer these questions:
   (a) What interests you? What do you enjoy doing?
   (b) What concerns you?
   (c) What *haven't* you considered?
4. As you make choices, ask if those choices will materially and sustainably contribute to your ability to achieve happiness.

Chapter Five

If You Choose to Pursue a College Degree, Here's the Goal You Need to Set

It is quite possible that your answers to the questions posed in the previous chapter have led you to conclude that obtaining a college degree is the right decision for you. That's fine! Let's now make sure your college experience is successful, so college doesn't ruin your life.

By now, you have articulated your goal properly. You don't merely want to go to college. You want to get a college degree. But that's actually insufficient.

So, I urge you to set this as your goal:

"My goal is to graduate from college in four years, debt-free, on the dean's list, with a degree that allows me to have a career in the field I want to work in."

Let's examine each of the key words and phrases in that goal statement.

Graduate from college. As you now understand, attending college is merely part of the journey that will take you to the career you want. What matters, then, is not going to college but graduating with a degree.

But that's not enough. You must not only graduate; you must graduate **in four years.** You'll learn why this is so important in Chapter 7; for now, I'll just say that few undergrads accomplish this goal anymore, and their failure costs them more than $1 million over their career.[1]

You must not only graduate in four years; you must graduate **debt-free.** Otherwise, you'll be saddled with financial strife that will definitely interfere with, possibly harm and perhaps even destroy your post-college life. Emerging from college with student loan debt will delay and could prevent you from living the life you envision (or merely assume you'll eventually have). Yet 70% of those who graduated from college in 2024 left school with student loans, and the

---

[1] Yeah, I know that sentence is tempting you to skip over to Chapter 7, but don't. Proceed to the next sentence instead.

average debt was $41,530, according to the Department of Education. Americans now owe more in student debt ($1.8 trillion) than auto loans ($1.7 trillion) and credit cards ($1.2 trillion). Only indebtedness to mortgages ($12.6 trillion) is bigger, say the Peter G. Peterson Foundation, Lending Tree, Trading Economics and the Education Data Initiative.

The impact of all this student debt is clear:

- The median age of first-time homebuyers in 1981 was 29. Today it's 38, says the National Association of Realtors. Those with student loans need 10 years on average to accumulate enough money to make a down payment on a home. That's twice as long as it takes students who graduate without debt, according to Apartment List.
- In 1990, 67% of Americans 30 years old were married. In 2024, only half were, according to the Aspen Economic Strategy Group.
- The percentage of women aged 30 who have ever given birth has fallen 10% since 1990, to 71%. And nearly half (47%) of childless adults under 50 say they are unlikely to ever have kids.
- Nearly 9% of 30- to 40-year-olds still live with their parents, a 50% increase since 1990.

So, yeah, it's essential that you emerge from college without any student loan debt – and you'll discover how to do that in Chapter 9.

But as important as it is to graduate in four years debt-free, it's not enough. You must also graduate **on the dean's list**. As you'll see in Chapter 5, achieving this goal will enable you to get more from your degree, significantly improving its value to you.

Finally, along with graduating in four years, debt-free and on the dean's list, you must obtain a degree that **allows you to have a career in the field you want to work in.** This matters because there's much more to life than just making money.

That's why this book isn't about college. It's about being happy. That means being able to create and maintain the lifestyle you want, so we'll explore that next.

 Key Takeaway

1. If you choose college, this is the goal you must set for yourself: "Graduate from college in four years, debt-free, on the dean's list, with a degree that allows me to have a career in the field I want to work in."

Chapter Six

In Truth, College Is Really About Lifestyle

What are your aspirations?

Don't tell me that you want to travel and see new places, buy a car, get married, own a home and have children. Everyone says stuff like that.

Instead, frame all your endeavors in the context of *lifestyle*.

When you travel, do you want to:

- Stay at a midtown Manhattan three-star hotel like a Mariott Courtyard (a room was $268 per night in 2025) or a five-star hotel like the Four Seasons ($1,048; suites for $5,000)?

- Fly economy class ($127 from New York to Miami via United Airlines) or business class ($722)?
- Use public transportation ($3) or rent a car ($229 per week for a Chevy Spark from Hertz, or $2,520 per week for a Mercedes SL-Class from Pugachev Luxury Rentals)?
- Eat at fast-food joints (less than $10) or dine at the Michelin two-star restaurant L'Atelier de Joël Robuchon ($466 per person)?

You get my point. Almost everything you'll do in life will involve – and require – money. Most people get a job and then build a lifestyle based on what that income will permit. This is completely wrong. What you should do instead is figure out how much your desired lifestyle will cost and then get a job that gives you the ability to earn enough income to pay those costs.

But few people do that. Instead, they focus on the career they want and then passively accept whatever salary they get as the price of pursuing that career. But their passivity, their tolerance of that limited income, often doesn't last. For example, education majors know that schoolteachers don't earn much money compared to most careers, but they love kids and want to devote their careers to teaching. So, they consign themselves to living the lifestyle of teachers.

Except lots of them can't sustain it. More than 300,000 schoolteachers quit in the 2022–2023 school year, according to the American Educational Research Association, and McKinsey says the number-one reason is compensation.

If you're thinking, "Well, that'll never be me. I love my chosen field and will remain dedicated to it even if my salary isn't the greatest," then I have a quick quiz for you.

If you want to purchase something and you don't earn enough money to pay for it in full, will you:

(a) Not buy it and do without
(b) Buy something less expensive that you can afford
(c) Buy it and pay for it later, by using credit cards or other loans

It's easy to say you'll never choose option C. But how realistic is that assertion?

Say you agree to be in a close friend's wedding party. The bride or groom later says their bachelor or bachelorette party is going to be a weekend in New Orleans, Austin, Nashville or Las Vegas. Participating will cost you $1,000 – money you don't have and can't afford. Will you truly refrain from Option C?

Such are the dilemmas that life throws our way. So, please think a lot about the lifestyle you want, and investigate whether your planned career path can let you live it. If it can't, you'll have to change either your lifestyle or your career, as hundreds of thousands of schoolteachers are discovering every year.

Don't Forget Taxes

The average cost of a one-week vacation for two people in 2024 was $3,982, according to Bankrate. This includes airfare, hotel, ground transportation, three daily meals, plus typical expenses for admission fees, gifts and memorabilia.

Actually, that amount is not correct. The real cost is actually $5,688. Why so much more? Because of taxes. Here's why, assuming a combined 30% federal and state income tax rate:

Income	$5,688
30% paid in taxes	– 1,706
Income after taxes	**$3,982**

Although this is not a book on taxes, keep this in mind: *It's not what you earn that counts; it's what you keep after taxes.* And you're going to incur many kinds of taxes: income taxes, sales taxes, property taxes, use taxes, capital gains taxes, gift and estate taxes and more.

(If no adult has ever talked to you about taxes, it's time you had a conversation with some of them. Because you might get excited about getting a job that pays you $80,000 a year – until you realize you may lose $24,000 of it to income taxes, leaving you with just $56,000.)

For example, if you stay at a hotel in Miami Beach, you'll pay a 4% resort tax, a 3% convention development tax, a 2% tourist development tax and a 1% professional sports facilities franchise tax. So, even though the hotel says the room costs $400 a night, you'll actually spend $440 a night. Add a 2% food and beverage tax, unless you plan on fasting during your vacation.

Everything Costs More Than You Think

The average new automobile costs $47,542, according to Edmunds. But you'll actually spend much more than that. First, most states charge a sales tax; the average is 5% of the purchase price, or $2,377 for the average new auto. You'll also pay dealer preparation fees, destination fees, documentation fees, title and registration fees and auto insurance. (The average annual cost of auto insurance is $2,670, according to Bankrate.) The result? The average cost of a new auto is $52,589 – and you haven't even driven it yet!

Every mile you drive reduces the car's resale value and increases its maintenance and repair costs. Add the costs of gasoline, parking and tolls, and it's easy to see why AAA says the average American driver spends $9,282 annually on their truck or car.

Do you suppose you might get married one day? The average cost of a wedding in 2024 was $35,000, according to The Knot. This includes the wedding dress, tuxedos, venue rental, band or disc jockey, food and beverages, wedding cake, invitations, flowers, photographer and videographer and wedding planner. This figure, however, does not include the cost of the honeymoon (see the average vacation cost earlier), for a total cost of nearly $40,000.

Then there's homeownership, long called "the American Dream." The average homebuyer in 2024 paid $419,200 for a house, according to the Federal Reserve Bank of St. Louis. Even though you'll borrow money to buy that house (the loan is called a *mortgage*), you'll still need to pay 3% to 20% of the purchase price in cash (the *down payment*). That's $12,570 to $83,800.

You'll also be required to hire a title settlement company, which will charge a fee to conduct a title search (to confirm that the seller has the legal right to sell you the house), and then you'll buy title insurance (to protect you in case the title search later proves faulty). You'll also hire an appraiser (to confirm that the house is worth the price you're paying for it) and a home inspector (who will tell you if there are problems with the house that could force you to incur large costs after you move in, like replacing the roof). Add it up and you'll discover that homebuyers pay 3% to 6% ($12,500 to $25,000) in closing costs, in addition to the price of the house.

And you still haven't moved in! Be prepared to pay for a moving van or movers. You'll also want to buy furniture and everything from audio/video gear to household appliances to a lawn mower – not to mention draperies, liners for the kitchen cabinets, shower curtains and whatnot.

Sharing space in that dream of a house might be the pitter-patter of children. The cost of raising them? A middle-class couple will spend $300,000 per child from birth to age 17, for housing, food, clothing, health care, child care and more – everything from diapers to sports equipment – according to inflation-adjusted data from the U.S. Department of Agriculture. That's $17,647 per year, $1,470 per month, $367 per week, $53 per day, per child. Having three kids triples the cost.

And that's before you pay the cost of sending any of your kids to college.

All these items – travel, cars, weddings, homes, kids – comprise your lifestyle. And money is its foundation. So, let's look at the incomes of American households, courtesy of the 2023 Consumer Expenditure Survey produced by the federal government's Bureau of Labor Statistics. I've summarized the data for you in four income ranges, as shown in Table 6.1.

Table 6.1   Incomes of U.S. Households

	U.S. Households Annual Incomes of			
	Less Than $40,000	$40,000 to $99,999	$100,000 to $199,999	$200,000 or More
Income after taxes	$ 22,210	$ 59,418	$ 127,994	$ 259,392
College grad %	53%	67%	83%	94%
Homeowner %	47%	61%	80%	88%
Value of owned home	$ 149,062	$ 225,387	$ 383,351	$ 697,287

There's a bounty of useful insights in these data that can really help you choose your post-high school path. For example, the previous information reveals that:

- Almost every household (94%) earning more than $200,000 is headed by a college graduate. Sure, it's possible to make a lot of money without a degree, but only 6% of adults manage to pull that off – and most of them are professional athletes (think Lionel Messi), Hollywood stars (Tom Cruise), top recording artists (Taylor Swift), best-selling authors (JK Rowling) or ground-breaking entrepreneurs (Mark Zuckerberg). If such paths are unlikely for you, then so are the chances that you'll earn $200,000+ without a degree.
- Shockingly, more than half of those earning under $40,000 have a college degree! *WHAAAAAT???!!!* You can speculate as well as I can as to why this might be, but this surely helps

explain why half of college graduates have a negative opinion of the value of college.
- The more money you earn, the more likely you are to own your home, and the more valuable that home is. This is important: With a college degree, not only are you more likely to live in a nicer home in a nicer neighborhood, but your home's value will rise more than the homes owned by people who earn far less than you. This helps explain why those with a college degree tend to become wealthier over time than people without degrees.

Next, let's see how much money each of these groups spend, shown in Table 6.2. You won't be surprised to see that the more money people earn, the more money they spend, but this chart contains lots of surprises, nevertheless.

Here we find even more valuable insights. Examine the data closely, and you'll see that:

- On average, those earning an average of just $22,210 (Table 6.1) are spending an average of $33,655 (Table 6.2) – 52% more than their income! How is that possible? The answer: They get a lot of money from the government. (Some people call this "support," while others call these "handouts.") Government programs that give money to low-income households include:
  a. Half a million adults and 1.5 million children receive welfare, formally called **Temporary Assistance for Needy Families**. The average monthly check per household is $650, and recipients can spend the money however they want.

Table 6.2 How Americans Spend Their Money

	U.S. Households with Annual Incomes of			U.S. Households with Annual Incomes of		
	Less Than $40,000	$40,000 to $99,999	$100,000 to $199,999	$200,000 or More	Less Than $40,000	$40,000 to $99,999	$100,000 to $199,999	$200,000 or More
	Average Annual Expenses				As Percent of After-Tax Income			
Housing	$ 7,331	$ 10,265	$ 16,794	$ 42,559	33.0%	17.3%	13.1%	16.4%
Pensions/Social Security	$ 893	$ 4,656	$ 14,894	$ 31,127	4.0%	7.8%	11.6%	12.0%
Transportation	$ 5,900	$ 10,444	$ 18,895	$ 28,308	26.6%	17.6%	14.8%	10.9%
Health care	$ 3,803	$ 5,546	$ 7,656	$ 10,711	17.1%	9.3%	8.0%	4.1%
Food at home	$ 4,030	$ 5,462	$ 7,838	$ 9,702	18.2%	9.2%	6.1%	3.7%
Entertainment	$ 1,780	$ 2,529	$ 4,939	$ 9,526	8.0%	4.3%	3.9%	3.7%
Food away from home	$ 1,813	$ 3,011	$ 5,775	$ 8,824	8.2%	5.1%	4.5%	3.4%
Education	$ 218	$ 704	$ 1,846	$ 6,804	1.0%	1.2%	1.4%	2.6%

(Continued)

Table 6.2 (Continued)

	U.S. Households with Annual Incomes of				U.S. Households with Annual Incomes of			
	Less Than $40,000	$40,000 to $99,999	$100,000 to $199,999	$200,000 or More		Less Than $40,000	$40,000 to $99,999	$100,000 to $199,999	$200,000 or More
	Average Annual Expenses					As Percent of After-Tax Income			
Utilities	$ 3,238	$ 4,403	$ 5,645	$ 6,727		14.6%	7.4%	4.4%	2.6%
Cash contributions	$ 943	$ 1,749	$ 2,698	$ 6,461		4.2%	2.9%	2.1%	2.5%
Clothing	$ 1,057	$ 1,559	$ 2,741	$ 4,671		4.8%	2.6%	2.1%	1.8%
Miscellaneous	$ 548	$ 1,107	$ 1,533	$ 2,375		2.5%	1.9%	1.2%	0.9%
Personal care	$ 495	$ 797	$ 1,276	$ 1,905		2.2%	1.3%	1.0%	0.7%
Cellular phone service	$ 774	$ 1,219	$ 1,686	$ 1,769		3.5%	2.1%	1.3%	0.7%
Alcoholic beverages	$ 259	$ 409	$ 1,054	$ 1,567		1.2%	0.7%	0.8%	0.6%
Life insurance	$ 189	$ 371	$ 719	$ 1,496		0.9%	0.6%	0.6%	0.6%
Tobacco	$ 385	$ 411	$ 350	$ 221		1.7%	0.7%	0.3%	0.1%
	$ 33,655	$ 54,640	$ 96,335	$ 174,753		151.7%	92.0%	77.2%	67.2%
Spending as a Percent of After-Tax Income	152%	92%	75%	67%					

b. Twenty-two million households get $400 per month in food stamps, called the **Supplemental Nutrition Assistance Program**. They use this money to buy groceries.
c. **Low-Income Home Energy Assistance Program** pays the monthly utility bills for 15 million households nationwide.
d. Nearly five million households qualify for **Housing Choice Vouchers** (formerly called Section 8 housing). They pay up to 30% of their income on rent, and the government pays the rest. The program costs taxpayers $32 billion per year, or an average of $6,400 per household.
e. The government spent $12 billion on **Head Start** in 2023, a program that provides free day care and other services for about one million children up to age five of low-income families. That's about $12,000 per child.
f. The **Earned Income Tax Credit** is a tax refund to low- and moderate-income taxpayers. It's called a "refund" even though most recipients don't pay any taxes. More than 48 million people receive an average of $529 each year via this program.
g. All taxpayers with children under 17 qualify for the **Child Tax Credit**; the lower your income, the larger the credit. The average credit per taxpayer in 2022 was $2,390; the total cost of the program was $122 billion.

There are still more tax credits, including family and dependent credits, income and savings credits, homeowner credits and health care credits, child and dependent care tax credits, and the American Opportunity Tax Credit, but you get the point. The question you want to ask yourself is: Do you want a meager lifestyle that depends on government support? If so, you can skip college and apply for the previously mentioned programs instead.

- Even those earning $40,000 to $99,000 are spending almost as much as they earn – something known as "living paycheck to paycheck." People in this income group earn too much to qualify for government subsidies, so they rely on their parents for help. And I'm not talking solely about 20-somethings who are just out of college. According to a study by Savings.com, half (50%) of parents are providing financial support to at least one of their adult children; the average is $1,474 per month. Table 6.3 shows you the amount and type of support Mom and Dad are providing.

  Think about that: If you need help paying your bills but are going into debt because you can't get that help, how can you save and invest for the future? The answer is that most can't. More than a third of U.S. adults (38%) don't own any stocks, and the median savings of Baby Boomers is just $289,000, according to Investopedia. That's not even enough to generate $1,000 a month in retirement income. You need to set yourself on a path that lets you avoid this fate.

- And that path means entering a career that lets you earn more than $100,000 per year. Those earning $100,000 to $199,999 have 25% of their incomes left over after paying their bills, and those earning $200,000+ have 33% of their incomes left over, meaning they have plenty of cash to save and invest. That's how they're able to create wealth over time. (Yep, the rich get richer, while the poor stay poor.)

Table 6.3 How Parents Financially Support Their Adult Children

Category	% of parents providing support to adult children	Average monthly support provided
Groceries or food	83%	$ 220
Cell phone	63%	$ 63
Rent or mortgage	62%	$ 653
Health insurance or health care	50%	$ 165
Leisure/vacations	44%	$ 190
Discretionary spending	44%	$ 126
Car	44%	$ 218
Tuition or other school expenses	42%	$1,198
Student loans	22%	$ 226
Credit cards	21%	$ 160

- Perhaps the most important takeaway from this chart: It reveals why lower-income households struggle so hard to save, compared to households with higher incomes. Look closely at the right-hand side of the chart; it shows you each income group's spending as a percentage of their income. As you can see, the higher your income, the less of it you spend on each category, in percentage terms.

This is because Big Macs cost the same whether you're rich or poor. President Donald Trump loves Big Macs, and he pays the same price for them as you do – but as a percentage of his income and wealth, they surely must seem to him that they're free.

Households earning under $40,000, for example, spend 27% of their incomes on transportation, while households earning $200,000 or more spend only 11%, or nearly two-thirds less in percentage terms. And that's despite the fact that richer households are driving nicer, more expensive vehicles!

Spend some time with these two charts and see what other conclusions you can reach.

It's easy to get discouraged, or even angry, at the fact that lower-income households are so burdened by today's high cost of living. Although it's not their fault that automobiles are so expensive, let's not dismiss too quickly the control that people do have over their lives. For example, no one says you must purchase a new vehicle when used ones are readily available at far lower cost (the average used car that's three years old costs less than $28,000, compared to nearly $50,000 for the average new vehicle, according to Cox Automotive).

Those with low incomes (and generally less education) spend nearly 2% of their annual income on tobacco; those who are better educated spend virtually nothing on this terribly unhealthy habit. Not only are higher-income people putting their money to better use, being tobacco-free lowers their cost of health insurance (which frees up yet more cash), and their better health reduces their overall health care spending (freeing up yet even more cash). And they feel better! A virtuous cycle!

Life is all about choices, and you're in the very moment where you're about to make some of the most important choices of your life.

The information in these charts can help you make the right ones. When it comes to college, cost is one of the most important factors in your effort to make the right choice. So, let's examine the cost of college next.

 Key Takeaways

1. Frame all your endeavors in the context of *lifestyle*. Think about what you must *give* so you can *get* the benefits offered by a given career. Is the trade-off acceptable to you?
2. Don't forget taxes. Your income net of taxes is what matters, not your gross pay. You'll likely lose about a third of your income to federal and state taxes, so keep that in mind when making financial decisions.
3. Everything costs more than you expect. Additional fees and unexpected costs are unavoidable, so be sure to increase your assumptions about how much you'll spend – on everything from dinners out to buying a home.
4. Life is all about choices, and you're in the very moment where you're about to make some of the most important choices of your life. So take your time, be deliberative, and consider the comments of others – but in the end, it's your decision. Only you will live with the consequences.

Chapter Seven

The Cost of College

To receive a college degree, you must obtain 120 qualifying college credits.[1]

Generally, you are awarded college credits each time you get a passing grade when completing a qualifying course. Most courses reward you with three college credits. (Some classes generate more, others less.)

As in high school, most college classes award the grades A, B, C, D or F. But here's an important point: Whether you get an A or a D, you get the same three credits. This causes some students to mistakenly believe that there's no reason to work harder for that A grade. Why not just do the minimal work to get a C? You'll have more time

---

[1] By "qualifying" I mean that the credits must be approved by your school and pertain to the degree you're seeking. As you'll soon see, not all the credits that students obtain qualify.

to party – and you'll still get the same degree as the student who got straight As. (There's a joke they tell in hospitals: *What do you call the student who graduates at the bottom of the class in medical school?*[2])

I'll explain later why getting that A matters. First, let's continue our conversation about college credits.

Most colleges offer two semesters per year: Fall and Spring. Table 7.1 adds it up for you.

Since you generally need 120 credits to graduate, this means it will take you four years to get your degree.

That's the *time* cost of getting a degree. Now, let's look at the *money* cost.

The least expensive colleges in the country are those operated by state governments; their average cost of tuition and fees for *in-state* students (meaning those who live in the state) for the 2024–2025 academic year was $406 per credit, according to the Education Data Initiative. Since each class awards three credits, that means you'll pay $1,218 per class, or $6,090 for five classes per semester. And because you'll attend two semesters each year, you'll spend a total of $12,180 per year on tuition and fees.

Table 7.1 Getting 30 College Credits Per Year

Semesters per year	2
Classes per semester	x 5
Credits per class	x 3
	30 credits earned per year

---

[2] "Doctor."

That's not the total cost you'll incur, however. You'll also pay an average of $1,530 for books and supplies each year ($153 per class). Living on campus and eating in the school's dining hall (together called *room and board*) costs an average of $12,984 per year. And other miscellaneous expenses add up to $4,140 per year, says EDI.

Thus, the grand total to attend an in-state public college or university in the 2024–2025 academic year was $30,834.

So, what is the total cost of getting a degree? You might be thinking the answer is $123,336 ($30,834 x four years). But that's incorrect.

Here's why. That $30,834 is the cost to attend college in 2024–2025. But that's not the cost for the year after that, because college costs rise every year. From 1977 to 2024, in fact, college costs rose an average of 6.1% per year, according to the Bureau of Labor Statistics. At that rate, your sophomore year would cost $32,715, your junior year would cost $34,711 and your senior year would cost $36,828.

Thus, the total cost for the four years would be $135,088.

And even that figure isn't right. Why not? Because the average full-time student earns just 22 credit hours per year, according to the National Student Clearinghouse. At that pace, it takes six years to graduate, not four. Only 28% of students earn enough credits each year to graduate in four years.

Why do 7 in 10 students fail to graduate in four years? There are three main reasons. First, they sometimes fail their courses (NCS says the average course load is 27 credits but only 22 are earned). Second, most take only four classes each semester, thus collecting only 96 credits in four years. That's 24 credits short of what they need for a degree, forcing them to spend another two years at college to complete their degree requirements.

Third, students often end up receiving 150 credits – far more than the 120 needed to graduate. Why would a student pay for more credits than needed? Because 80% of students change their majors and 37% transfer to a different school, says the National Student Clearinghouse.

When you change your major, the classes you took in your former major don't apply, meaning the time and money you spent are wasted. As a result, you end up taking more classes than if you'd selected the right major at the beginning of your college journey. And if you transfer to another school, the new institution is likely to reject some or all of the credits you earned at the prior institution – forcing you to retake the same classes, resulting in more time and money to get your degree. It's true: Studies by both the General Accountability Office and the National Student Clearinghouse found that students lose an average of 43% of their credits when transferring to another school.

Students who change majors and/or schools rarely consider the financial impact of their decisions. But the impact is *huge*. By failing to graduate in four years, you're forced to attend college in years five and six, and the cost rises every year. This is why it's vital that you get 15 credits each semester, not just 12.

It's equally vital that you stick with your initial major and school. But how likely is that? You might not yet know what field you want to pursue. You might discover a different path while in college. I'm not saying you have to feel that you're stuck with your initial choice. But I am saying that the later you make the switch or the more often you choose majors or schools, the longer it'll take you to graduate and the more you'll spend obtaining the degree. All this means you must choose carefully – and if you aren't confident that your initial choice will prove correct, then you probably shouldn't go to college just yet. Delay for a year or two, and use the time to figure it out.

After all, if you end up having to attend college for two additional years, assuming the aforementioned historical rate of college inflation, the fifth year of college will cost $39,074 and the sixth year will cost $41,458. That brings the total cost over six years to $215,620; you'll have spent $80,532 in the last two years alone!

And if you think spending an extra eighty grand is awful, it's even worse than you think! Those two extra years will really cost you close to $600,000!

Here's why. Not only must you pay the costs of tuition, room and board, books and miscellaneous expenses for an extra two years, you're going to borrow even more money in student loans – and that means you'll spend a lot more in interest over the next 20 years. Even worse, it means you lose two years of being in the workplace; instead of graduating at age 22, you won't graduate until age 24. If you earn $50,000 upon graduation, delaying graduation by two years translates into two years of lost income and thus two years of lost savings and investments. By my calculations, graduating in six years means you'll enter retirement with nearly $600,000 less than the student who graduates in four years.

It's Even More Costly to Attend Out-of-State and Private Colleges and Universities

All the numbers I've shown pertain to attendance at public institutions for in-state students. If you attend a public school in a different state or a private college or university, you'll spend massively more amounts of money.

For the 2024–2025 academic year, the average cost for an out-of-state student (meaning you're attending a public school that's not in the state where you live) was $55,070. Getting the degree in four years costs $241,268. If you take six years to get the degree, the cost would be $385,099.

Private colleges and universities are the most expensive of all, as shown in Table 7.2: an average of $67,538 for the 2024–2025 academic year. Over four inflation-adjusted years, that's $295,892. Or, if it takes you six years, $381,480.

It should be obvious to you by now: Don't overpay for your college degree. Less obvious, though, is what I mean by "don't overpay." So, let me elaborate for you.

First, obtain those 120 credits as fast as possible, because the sooner you finish, the less you pay and the sooner you can enter the workforce and start earning an income. I finished college in 3½ years, by taking both summer and *winter session* classes (short, four-week

Table 7.2 The Cost of College

| | The Cost of College | |
| | Completing Your Degree in | |
	4 Years	6 Years
Public In-State School	$135,088	$215,620
Public Out-of-State School	$241,268	$385,099
Private School	$295,892	$381,480

Source: Education Data Initiative.

courses held during the Christmas/New Year's break). I also earned 18 credits (via six courses) in some semesters instead of the usual 15.[3]

Second, choose as inexpensive a school as possible. Third, select a major that leads to a high-paying job. Both these points demand more commentary, so let's explore them in the next chapter.

 Key Takeaways

1. College costs rise every year, and the rate of increase is usually higher than the nation's overall inflation rate. This is why you need to graduate in as little time as possible – because your first year's costs will be almost a third cheaper than your sixth year.
2. You'll spend far more to get a degree from an out-of-state or private college or university than if you attend a public in-state institution.

---

[3] My record: a whopping 24 credit hours in one semester. But that landed me in the hospital, so I can't say I recommend this. But I got the credits!

Chapter Eight

The Most Important College Choices You'll Make

F ive years after graduating, says the New York Federal Reserve, people with a degree in engineering earn an average of $73,000, while those with a degree in psychology earn an average of $40,000. This pay disparity is not surprising. But here's the thing: at any given college or university, *both degrees typically cost the same to obtain.*

Indeed, some degrees simply offer a low ROI – *return on investment*. Your investment is massive: four years of your life, plus maybe $300,000. This is a huge financial investment, and you must make sure you get an economic return worthy of it.

This is a huge point – perhaps the most important, and distinctive, in this entire book. That's because many people believe that income-earned-after-graduation doesn't matter. They argue that college is mostly about personal enrichment, that you should follow your passion, that your degree should help you make the world a better place.

Bullshit.

Maybe that viewpoint was valid 75 years ago, back in the 1960s when few people went to college (meaning *any* degree set you apart) and when the average 4-year degree, says the National Center for Education Statistics, cost just $5,425 – not per class or semester; that was for the entire degree!

Today, of course, the situation is far different. Nearly two-thirds (61%) of high school graduates go to college, according to the Bureau of Labor Statistics. That means you've got a lot more competition for jobs than college grads did in the 1960s. And the cost of getting that degree is massively more expensive. All this adds up to one undeniable fact: It is more important than ever that your degree lead to a high-paying income to justify its cost (especially if you must use student loans to pay for college, more about this later).[1]

---

[1] While the cost of a degree in 1963–1967 was $5,245, the average income for 1967 graduates was $8,312, according to the National Association of Colleges and Employers. Thus, in their first year out of school, graduates earned an average 1.6 times more than what they spent to get their degree. That's one helluva ROI. But by 2024, the average graduate salary of $68,516 was only 0.3 times the average $187,612 cost of their degree. The sharply lower ROI for today's graduates reflects the fact that the cost of college has grown far faster than salary increases. The ROI is so low, in fact, that you have to wonder if it's really worth it.

Look, I'm not trying to denigrate the idea that you follow your passion. You truly should. It's just that your passion should be an avocation, not your career pursuit. Got a passion? Great! Make it your hobby or a side gig – something you devote time and attention to *after* you've finished your day at work. Or pursue your passion without spending four years and a couple hundred grand on it. There are now thousands of excellent online courses in hundreds of subjects, at little to no cost, offered by dozens of educational institutions – the very same institutions that students pay hundreds of thousands of dollars to attend.

The sad reality is that too many well-meaning adults are thinking about what college was like when they went to college decades ago. Too often they ignore or are oblivious to the economic reality that you're facing today. If you pursue a degree that doesn't lead to sufficient economic reward, you could easily ruin your life.

If College Is a Money Pit, Student Loans Are the Shovel

Ruination is made even more likely if you obtain student loans to pay for college. This is a very important point, because student loans are astonishingly common. More than half of all students (54%) get loans, and they leave college with an average debt of $41,520, according to the Education Data Initiative. Truly, those loans will ruin your life.

Don't believe me? A 2024 survey by Lumina Foundation found that 71% say their student debts have forced them to delay:

- Buying a car
- Buying a house
- Getting married
- Having children
- Moving out of their parents' home
- Starting a business

This is why, according to Lumina, 78% of U.S. adults say college is not worth the cost. And Best Colleges found that 6 in 10 (61%) graduates would choose a different major if given the opportunity for a do-over. The main reason, they say, is to get into a field offering better job opportunities and compensation.

So, this is your opportunity to learn from their mistake: Decide now that you will attend an inexpensive college or university. Then, select the right major and avoid accumulating student loans.

It's tragic that most students fail to follow this advice. Yet, it's easy to see how they (and the adults guiding them) fall into the trap of seeking and accepting student loans. For one thing, student loans are so common – 43 million Americans have them – that everyone has come to believe they are unavoidable and even benign.

But they are neither. Quite the opposite. That's because student loans operate differently from every other kind of loan. Let's explore this to help you understand why you must stay away from student loans.

Understanding Student Loans

To begin with, I'm not condemning indebtedness. Loans are an important part of our lives, and necessarily so. Without loans, people can't buy cars or houses. Entrepreneurs can't start businesses. Farmers can't grow crops. Governments can't serve their citizens or defend their nations. All rely on loans to obtain the money they need to achieve their goals. And it all makes sense: You might not have $500,000 to buy a house, but thanks to the income you earn, you can afford the monthly payment on the loan, allowing you to buy that house.

When asked to provide a loan, lenders ask borrowers three simple questions:

1. What will you do with the money we lend you?
2. How will you repay the money?
3. How can we get our money back if you fail to repay us?

These questions are easily answered by most borrowers. If your parents sought a loan to buy a home (called a *mortgage*), here's how they answered those questions:

1. "We are going to use the money you lend us to purchase the house."
2. "One or both of us have jobs, and we're going to use our income(s) to make the loan's monthly payment."
3. "We will post the house as collateral. Thus, if we don't make the payments each month (because we've lost our jobs, or due to any other reason), you can sell the house to get your money back."

These are good answers, and they give the lender comfort that its risk is low. And to make its risk even lower, lenders take two important steps: First, it doesn't lend your parents 100% of the house's price. Instead, it lends only 80% of the value. Thus, your parents are required to pay 20% in cash. For a $400,000 home, for example, the lender would provide $320,000, and your parents would pay $80,000 as a *down payment*. Second, the lender gives the money being lent to the home's seller, not your parents.

These tactics give the lender three benefits. First, if the lender has to cancel the loan (called *foreclosure*) because your parents don't make the payments, the lender only needs to sell that $400,000 house for $320,000 to get its money back. Second, by lending only $320,000 to your parents instead of $400,000, it can lend that extra $80,000 to other borrowers – and the more loans it makes, the less risk it takes and the more money it makes.[2] Third, giving the loan amount directly to the seller means your parents never have control over the funds – and this prevents them from using the money for a different purpose.

You might have missed the most important point in all of this. In fact, I am certain that you have. I say that because I've quizzed thousands of homeowners about this point over three decades, and no one has ever gotten this point correct. Yet it is crucial to helping you understand how loans work – and in the context of this book, this point enables you to understand why student loans are so dangerous.

---

[2] It's less risk, because lending to 100 borrowers is safer than lending to just one. One or two loans might go into foreclosure, but it's not likely that all 100 will. And lenders charge fees to issue (*underwrite*) loans, so the more loans it underwrites, the more fees it earns.

So, allow me now to make the point for you, and I'll do so by giving you the same one-question quiz that I've asked thousands of homeowners. Ready? Here it is.

Fill in the blank: A mortgage is a loan against _____.

. . .

Is your answer, "the home"?

That answer is incorrect, yet it's the answer I always hear. The truth is that mortgages are *not* loans based on the value of the property. Rather, a mortgage is a loan against *the borrower's income.* As you can discern from question 2 in the lender's three-question qualification process, you will not get approved for a loan if you don't have an income.[3]

Here's the second part of the issue: Getting approved for a loan is only half the story. The other half is the interest rate the lender charges you for that loan. And the rate is based on the lender's risk of loaning you the money.

In the case of mortgages, the risk is low, partly because the borrower's income is enough to make the monthly payments and partly because the property is posted as collateral. This is why the interest rate on mortgage loans is in the single digits.

This is also why credit cards charge interest rates that average 21%. Credit card rates are high because no collateral is posted. Unlike a mortgage, which lets the lender take your house if you fail to make the monthly payments, a credit card company can't seize that sweater you bought or the beer you drank. Lack of collateral translates into

---

[3] Don't believe me? Then call a bank, say you're a teenager in high school with no job, and ask to borrow $400,000. When they decline your request, ask them why. You'll see that I'm right.

> Like all lenders, card issuers usually want proof that you have an income. But credit card companies are often willing to give credit cards to unemployed college students, on the theory that they will get good-paying jobs upon graduation and become lifelong customers. Until then, card companies reduce their risk by limiting the amount that students can borrow.

increased risk for the lender – and the lender compensates for its higher risk by charging card users higher rates of interest.[4]

This is how all home loans, auto loans, business loans and personal loans work. But it's not how student loans work – and that's why student loans are a deadly trap for college students.

Here's how student loans are different: First, when the student asks for a loan, the lender will provide it. All of it. If the school year costs $20,000, the lender will loan $20,000 – it won't demand that the student make a down payment. (Lenders sometimes even loan more than the cost of tuition and room and board – purportedly so the student can pay for books, transportation costs and more. Extending loans for indirect expenses never happens with any other type of loan.)

Second, the lender won't require the student to have an income. It will often provide the loan anyway.

---

[4] Although credit card companies charge an average of 21%, their revenues are a bit less. That's because, as of February 2025, 7.2% of cardholders hadn't made payments in the past 90 days (called *delinquency*). This is why card companies charge everyone higher rates – to offset the impact of those who don't repay their debts.

Third, lenders often don't require that students make any monthly payments until six months after graduation (some loan programs do require payments while you're in school).

Fourth – and this is the most awful difference of all – the lender will give the money being lent directly to the student, leaving it to the student to pay for tuition, room and board and related expenses.

Imagine! The lender is giving tens of thousands of dollars to 18-year-olds who have never seen such sums before. What will you do with this money when you get it?

Too many of your classmates do stupid things with their student loans. The most recent study I found on this, in 2016, found that 15% used their student loans to buy clothes, 13% spent the money at restaurants, 3% took vacations and another 3% spent the money on alcohol and drugs. There's no reason to believe that today's college students are behaving any differently.

The worst part: Lots of students drop out of school. Nearly a third (30%) concluded that college wasn't for them. Even more (32%) say family pressures caused them to quit. And the number-one reason why students dropped out of college (42% of them), according to the Education Data Initiative, is financial pressure (such as not having enough money to get something to eat, called *food insecurity*).

The result is that 16% of all U.S. adults – one in six – are college dropouts, says EDI. But the student loans that all those people got weren't conditioned on graduating. **If you drop out of college, you must still repay your student loans!**

And college dropouts have a lot of debt to repay: 39 million dropouts have college debt, and even though their average debt is half that of graduates ($14,000 versus $30,000), their default rate is higher.

Even though graduates owe twice as much, they also have two or three times the income, so they can afford to repay their debt more easily than dropouts can.

This brings us to the fifth way student loans differ from all other student loans: You can't discharge the loan by filing for bankruptcy. With every other type of loan, going bankrupt eliminates your obligation to repay the loan. Not so with student loans: You'll still have to repay them.

And that's a fact discovered in 2025 by two million people who have student loans. That's when the Education Department started garnishing the wages of borrowers who'd been in default on their student loans (meaning, they hadn't made payments in nine months or more). When your paycheck is *garnished* (meaning, seized), the government takes 15% of your pay until the debt is repaid.

> By the way, garnishments are coordinated through employer payroll. That means your employer will be told that you've defaulted on a debt – potentially creating an embarrassing and perhaps even career-threatening situation for you.

Transunion says six million people haven't made student-loan payments in 90 days or more, and the New York Federal Reserve says nine million borrowers have experienced a drop in their credit scores because of late- or non-payments. These numbers – delinquencies, defaults, garnishments and drops in credit scores – are likely to rise due to President Trump's 2025 Big Beautiful

Tax Bill Act, which requires the average student-loan borrower to pay $2,929 per year more in loan repayments than previously required, according to the Student Borrower Protection Center.

One final point about student loans: I said that lenders usually agree to give you a student loan even if you don't have an income. But some lenders do require that someone with an income co-sign your loan. By co-signing, they become legally responsible for repaying the loan if you fail to do so.

Nine in 10 student loans have been co-signed by the students' parents or grandparents, according to *Money* magazine. Nearly four million parents owed $65 billion to Parent PLUS Loans (provided by the federal government), an average of more than $16,000 per family, according to the National Center for Education Statistics, and nearly 200,000 retirees have had their Social Security checks garnished by the federal government because payments on student loan debts hadn't been made.

You don't want that to happen to your parents or grandparents, do you? Of course not. So, the burden is on you to make enough money so you can pay off your student loans – so they don't have to.

And that's why you must minimize the amount of debt you amass when going to college. One way, of course, is to get a grant or scholarship. But only 11% of students get them, and the average is just $15,750 – enough to cover only a third of the average cost of college. Thus, it's not only highly unlikely that you'll get any grants or scholarships (the odds are 9:1 that you won't), you'll probably still have to pay the other two-thirds of the cost of college, potentially causing you to seek student loans.

If student loans are unavoidable, you can minimize your indebtedness by doing two things: first, select an inexpensive college. Second, graduate in four years, because those who do accumulate one-third less debt ($30,000 on average) than those who graduate in six years ($45,000), according to EDI.

If you fail to follow this advice, you'll likely be saddled with student loan debt for decades. Indeed, 42% of all student loan borrowers are still paying off their loans 20 years after graduating; 25% of all student loans are held by Americans 50 and older, according to EDI. The National Consumer Law Center and New America report that 3.5 million Americans over age 60 have $125 billion in student loan debt.

The big message I'm hoping you get from this:

Avoid student loans so you can graduate debt-free.

 **Key Takeaways**

1. When choosing a major and a school, focus on the ROI – the return on investment. Is this the best use of hundreds of thousands of dollars and four or more years of your life?
2. Do everything you can to avoid amassing student loans so you can graduate debt-free.
   (a) The more debt you accumulate in college, the less you'll be able to borrow later to buy a car or home.

(b) If you drop out of college, you must still repay your student loans. This debt cannot be discharged by filing for bankruptcy.

(c) About 90% of student loans have been co-signed by parents or grandparents. If you have yours do this and you later don't repay the debt, they will be legally obligated to do so – even to the point of potentially having their Social Security retirement checks garnished by the federal government.

Chapter Nine

How to Minimize the Cost of Getting a College Degree

We've covered the basic rules you need to follow to prevent college from ruining your life. If you go to college, you must graduate in four years, debt-free, on the dean's list, with a degree that lets you enjoy a career in the field you want to work in.

The following strategies can help you achieve this goal.

1. Earn college credit by passing AP or DE classes in high school

Many high schools offer Advanced Placement or Dual Enrollment courses, which earn you college credit at hundreds of colleges and universities across the country. That cuts the time it takes to get your degree to as little as three years! That would not only reduce your cost of college by more than 25%, it would let you enter the workforce and begin your career twice as fast as most college students. This means you'd start saving and investing sooner, materially increasing your future wealth. (Consider identical high-school graduates who work until age 65, saving $500 per month throughout their careers, earning a 10% return per year.[1] The one who graduates after three years enters retirement with $1.1 million more than the one who takes six years to graduate.)

Although both AP and DE programs can lead to college credits, they differ in how they work. Deciding which is best for you depends on your goals, learning style and college plans. Let's look at each.

---

[1] That's the 100-year average annual return of the S&P 500 Stock Index.

AP Courses

Advanced Placement courses are college-level classes offered in high school and designed by the College Board, the same organization that administers the SAT college admissions test. AP classes are standardized nationwide and follow a prescribed curriculum that ends with a comprehensive exam that's administered each May.

There are about 40 AP subjects, ranging from STEM (such as AP Calculus and AP Physics) to humanities (AP U.S. History and AP English Literature) and the arts (AP Studio Art and AP Music Theory).

Every AP course ends with the AP Exam, and you'll score 1 to 5. Many colleges and universities award credit or advanced placement for scores of 3 or higher, while others require a 4 or 5. The exam score – not the course grade – determines whether you earn college credit.

Dual Enrollment Courses

These programs let high school students take actual college courses – at high school, a local college or online – and you earn credits for both high school and college simultaneously. Unlike AP, where college credit is determined by your score on the May exam, you get DE credit from the partnering college simply by passing the class.

DE programs are often available via state and community colleges, and tuition is often free or significantly reduced.

Table 9.1 compares AP and DE courses.

Table 9.1 Advanced Placement vs. Dual Enrollment

Feature	Advanced Placement	Dual Enrollment
Offered By	College Board	Colleges in partnership with high schools
Taught By	High school teachers with AP training	College instructors or certified high school teachers
College Credit Earned	Based on AP exam score	Based on course grade and passing status
Recognized Nationally?	Yes, widely recognized by U.S. colleges	Not all colleges accept programs
Transferability	More standardized across colleges	Depends on institution and location
Grading	One cumulative exam	Class assignments, tests, projects, etc.
Cost	About $100 per exam	Often free or low cost

Sources: College Board and Fairfax County VA Public Schools.

Which Option Is Better?

AP might be better for you if you are applying to competitive or out-of-state universities, perform well on standardized tests, want to demonstrate academic rigor in a nationally recognized format and are unsure which college you will attend and thus want portable credits.

DE might be better for you if you want a more project- or assignment-based grading system, prefer a guaranteed college transcript over a single high-stakes exam, plan to attend a public in-state college or community college that accepts DE credit and want a faster or more affordable pathway to earning college credits.

Some students take both AP and DE courses. From a college admissions perspective, both demonstrate that you're challenging yourself academically. But there's a risk to DE courses: because the grades go on your permanent college transcript, poor performance in a DE class will be part of your college record.

You can also earn college credit while in high school by joining the online site Study Hall, which lets you watch college courses from Arizona State University on YouTube and, for $400, obtain college credits that can be applied toward your degree at any college that accepts Arizona State credits.

2. Earn college credit by passing CLEP or DSST exams

The College-Level Examination Program lets you earn college credit for knowledge you obtained through self-study, work experience or independent learning. You receive the credits by passing exams created by the College Board (the same organization behind the SAT and AP). Each test lasts 90 minutes to two hours, and you can choose from three dozen subjects. Each exam costs less than $100. Many colleges grant three to six credits for passing scores. Learn more at clep.collegeboard.org.

DANTES Subject Standardized Tests are similar in structure and cost. Created for military service members, they're now available to everyone. The exams cover many subjects not included by CLEP. Learn more at getcollegecredit.com.

These programs are ideal for adult learners returning to school, military service members and veterans, homeschoolers or self-paced learners and students looking to skip intro classes, avoid college tuition costs and graduate faster.

3. Attend community college for the first two years

Let's be honest: Freshman year of college is little more than thirteenth grade. It's filled with general education (and sometimes, remedial) courses; freshmen don't take classes associated with their majors, so (academically speaking) you won't miss anything by going to community college.

By attending a local community college for two years, you'll earn an associate's degree. In almost every state, that guarantees you admission to one of the state's four-year colleges and universities. You'll still be able to get the B.A. or B.S. in four years, and you'll cut the cost of college almost in half, dramatically reducing the need for student debt.

Also, dispel any notions you have that community college represents an inferior education; nearly half (44%) of the nation's college students are enrolled at community colleges, according to the Department of Education. Besides, your bachelor's degree will still be from the four-year institution; that'll be the school you'll display on your résumé. If asked, you can easily explain that you chose to attend community college for the first two years for all the reasons cited earlier: It didn't interfere with your academic study yet saved you tens of thousands of dollars. Employers will be impressed by your reasoning (and wish they'd done it themselves). Trust me: Your community college experience won't harm your job prospects.

4. Choose a college or university that lets you get a degree tuition-free

You can get a free associate's degree from community colleges in 35 states; 25 states also offer free tuition at four-year schools offering bachelor's degrees. The other states are expected to offer similar programs in coming years, too.

Every tuition-free offer comes with details. At the University of Maryland, for example, you must be a Maryland resident and recipient of a Pell Grant. That federal program pays only a portion of tuition (see sidebar on next page), so UMD pays the rest. Since room and board costs another $15,000 a year, UMD will pay half that cost as well. California gives qualifying students $10,000 for tuition and living expenses in exchange for 450 hours of community service. Minnesota pays tuition and fees for students from families earning less than $80,000 a year. Dozens of states have similar programs.

If you hail from a low- to moderate-income household, you need to know about Pell Grants. They're administered by the Department of Education and represent the largest federal grant program available to college students.

Pell Grants can be used to pay for tuition and fees, as well as housing, books and other college costs. And you never repay the money you get (it's a grant, not a loan).

The maximum award for 2024–2025 was $7,395, and getting a grant doesn't reduce your eligibility for other aid. And almost every college in the country accepts Pell Grants. To apply, simply complete the student financial aid form known as FAFSA at Studentaid.gov.

Private colleges and universities are offering free education, too – including the elites: Brown, Columbia, Cornell, Dartmouth, Duke, Harvard, Johns Hopkins, MIT, Penn, Princeton, Stanford, Vanderbilt and Yale all provide free tuition to needy families. And how do they define "needy"? At MIT, it includes students whose families earn less than $200,000 a year. And if your family earns less than $100,000 a year, not only is tuition free, so are room and board, books and even personal expenses. It used to cost $86,000 a year to attend MIT; now, for most of its students, it's completely free. Ditto at dozens of schools.

5. If you're going to work part-time while attending college, do it for the right reasons

You're not likely to earn enough money in a part-time job to materially reduce your student loans. And every hour you spend commuting to work and working is an hour you're not studying or participating in extracurricular activities (where, frankly, you can learn as much as you do in classrooms) – harming your ability to get the most from your college investment.

On the other hand, working part-time demonstrates maturity and a great work ethic, two characteristics future employers love to see. So, if you're going to work part-time, get jobs that show future employers that you gained experience relevant to the job you're seeking. That's the best way to make part-time work worthwhile during your college years.

6. Consider working full-time and attending college part-time

Thousands of employers across the country will reimburse you for your tuition expenses. All you have to do is pass each course. In some cases, you must agree to stay with the employer for a few years following graduation.

Here's a sample of the employers offering to pay for your degree:

Amazon	Home Depot	Qualcomm
Boeing	Jeep/Chrysler/Fiat	Starbucks
Chase	JPMorgan Chase	Taco Bell
Chipotle	Lowe's	Target
Discover	Macy's	T-Mobile
Disney	Papa John's	Verizon
Fidelity	Publix	Walmart

and, of course, the U.S. Armed Forces

Some employers limit their tuition reimbursement program to degrees in fields that are important to them, so ask for details before you apply for a job with any given employer.

A detailed look at the education benefits offered by the U.S. Armed Forces

Extensive benefits are available when you enlist in the U.S. military. Here's what you can get:

For Active-Duty Personnel

- Up to $4,500 so you can take classes off-duty. Applicable for associate's, bachelor's and master's degrees, as well as licenses and certifications.

- Access to career counseling, testing and school options.
- Full-time internships/apprenticeships up to 180 days before you leave service, while still earning full pay from the military.

For Veterans
- The Post-9/11 GI Bill provides full public tuition, a housing stipend and $1,000/year for books. This is transferable to your spouse or children.
- A monthly stipend for on-the-job training and apprenticeships, which can be used for non-college training, such as plumbing, HVAC, law enforcement and union apprenticeships.
- The Yellow Ribbon Program pays for the extra tuition costs you'll incur if you attend a private or out-of-state school.
- The VA Work-Study Program provides a paid part-time job at VA locations while you're in school.
- VetSuccess on Campus gives you access to counselors who can help you get benefits and jobs.
- The Vocational Rehabilitation & Employment program offers tuition, counseling and job placement for disabled vets.

For Dependents
- The Transferred Post-9/11 GI Bill provides your children with the same GI Bill benefits that veterans get.
- The Yellow Ribbon Program covers tuition not paid by the GI Bill.
- The Fry Scholarship gives Post-9/11 GI Bill benefits to the children/spouses of fallen service members.

- DEA (Chapter 35) provides up to 45 months of payments for education/training to dependents of veterans who are deceased, MIA or 100% disabled due to service.
- MyCAA provides up to $4,000 for education/license costs for spouses of certain active-duty members.
- Survivors' and Dependents' Education Counseling is available through VA education counselors. They offer planning, benefits assistance and help with school selection.

There's more to learn about these options. If military service is of interest to you, each of the items shown is worth exploring.

The Reserve Officers' Training Corps program prepares you to become an officer in the U.S. military while you pursue your college degree. The program lets you major in any subject at 1,700 colleges and universities across the United States and adds military science courses, physical training and leadership development skills – plus generous financial benefits. It adds up to a unique opportunity to serve your country while earning valuable financial aid for college.

ROTC is available through the Army, Air Force (including the Space Force) and Navy (including the Marine Corps). In addition to classes devoted to your major, you'll take courses in military or naval science, leadership, ethics, military history and practical skills like communication and decision-making. You'll also participate in physical fitness training, field exercises and leadership labs. During the summer, you can attend advanced training courses or intern with military units.

Participating as a freshman and sophomore typically does not require any military commitment. If you continue as a junior and senior, you'll be eligible for scholarships that pay for tuition, fees and books, along with giving you a monthly allowance of $300 to $500 per month.

To get these financial benefits, you must agree to serve as a commissioned officer on active duty or in the Reserves or National Guard for four to eight years.

7. Select a school that's within a three-hour drive of home

Getting free tuition and room and board is great, but it's not enough. Pay attention to travel expenses, too – not just your own, but those of your family.

Sure, it's fun to envision attending a college that's thousands of miles from your overbearing parents and annoying younger siblings. And you probably daydream about a campus that's in a wonderful urban, mountain, rural or beach setting. But consider the transportation costs.

The farther away your school, the less often you'll be able to see your family. Maybe that's your point! But you can remain "away" even if the campus is 30 minutes from home. And regardless of the distance, you'll surely return home from school each Thanksgiving, December break, Spring break and summer recess. That's a minimum of four round-trips a year. If the school is a 30-minute drive from home, you'll spend a few bucks on gas and maybe a toll or two. But if you must fly, you'll spend thousands of dollars on travel expenses over the course of your college experience. ($200 airfare x four round-trip flights x six years = $4,800. Three trips by your parents adds $7,200, plus additional costs for their hotel, food and ground transportation.) Yup, selecting a college thousands of miles from home can easily cost an extra $12,000 or more – and no college or employer will reimburse these expenses.

I went to a college that was 30 minutes from my parents' home. Trust me: It was a world away. It can be for you, too.

8. Let's take this idea a step further, er, uh, closer: Consider living at home while you attend college

Don't dismiss this idea too quickly, because room and board represent more than half the cost of college.

Yeah, but you really want to live at school, right? I get it. But consider this: One in five young adults (19% of people ages 25–34) live at home, according to the National Association of Home Builders. And no wonder: More than half of Gen Z (52%) told Bank of America they can't afford to live the lifestyle they want.

Why live in a cramped one-bedroom apartment in a lousy part of town, where you have to traipse down to the basement to use a shared washer/dryer, pay for Netflix and utilities and shop for groceries that you must then cook and clean up afterward, when you can instead live in a beautifully furnished four-bedroom home in a quiet residential community, where Mom cooks your meals, does your laundry, cleans your room and lets you watch premium channels on a big-screen TV – all for free?

I doubt most young 20- and 30-somethings who are living with their parents are lazy. More likely, I suspect, is that living at home lets them divert most of their paycheck to savings and investments – accelerating their ability to one day buy a home of their own. This is really why your parents are happy to have you live with them during your early adult years. Besides, they like having you around. (Right?)

If you're going to live at home after you graduate, it's kind of difficult to argue that you need to spend $50,000 on a dorm or off-campus housing while you're in college.

9. Let's go furthest with this idea: Get a degree entirely through online courses

These days, you don't have to go to college; you can make college come to you.

Dozens of colleges and universities offer degrees that you obtain by taking all your classes online. Data is elusive, but it appears that upwards of 100,000 students get their degrees this way. And why not? It's far less expensive and far more convenient.

And it's not just virtual institutions that offer online degrees. So do dozens of traditional schools, including Arizona State, Boston University, Colorado State, Drexel, Georgetown, Northeastern, Oregon State, Penn State, Rowan University (of course), University of Florida, University of Illinois, University of Maryland, University of Massachusetts, Johns Hopkins and many more.

AP and DE classes. CLEP and DSST exams. Community college. Tuition-free degrees. Employer-paid tuition. Free housing. Online degrees. For most students, there is simply no way to justify paying a few hundred grand for a college degree when you can get one for far less – and even for free.

 **Key Takeaways**

1. Earn college credit by passing AP or DE classes, and by passing CLEP or DSST exams, while you're still in high school.
2. Attend community college for the first two years.
3. Choose a college or university that lets you obtain a degree tuition-free.
4. If you're going to work part-time while attending college, don't do it for the meager income you'll earn. Instead, do it because:
   (a) The job will let you associate with people who can be helpful in your future career pursuits.
   (b) Listing the job on your résumé will show future employers that you have the kind of work ethic they look for in job applicants.
5. Consider working full-time and attending college part-time.
6. Consider joining the military or ROTC.
7. The further from home your school is, the more you'll spend in transportation costs – potentially costing tens of thousands of dollars by the time you graduate. Therefore, select a school that's within a three-hour drive of home. Even consider living at home while you attend college.
8. Consider getting your degree online.

Chapter Ten

The 12 Biggest Mistakes Students Make

1. They rush into college

Is it smart to enroll in college even if you have no idea what career you want to pursue? Lots of adults say yes, arguing that the student will figure it out once they're there. No wonder, as cited earlier, three in four college freshmen are undeclared.

But adults who expect teens to figure it out are usually disappointed, because (again, as cited earlier) a quarter of freshmen drop out and only 62% graduate within six years. One of my clients spent $50,000 so their daughter could attend an out-of-state private school – only to watch her drop out after her freshman year. Fifty grand, gone. A year of the daughter's life, wasted.

If you know what you want to be when you grow up, great! Pursue that. But if you're as undecided as three in four high school seniors and college freshmen, then you should delay filing applications to college for a while. Maybe for a year or two, maybe for a decade. You wouldn't be alone: A third of college students are 25 and older, according to the Education Data Initiative, and nearly 10% are in their 30s. Another 4% are in their 40s, and 2% are age 50 or older. So, don't feel as though "everybody" goes to college right after high school. Half go to college much later.

You can benefit immensely by using the gap between high school and college (whether it's one year or several) to grow, develop and mature. Travel internationally. Get entry-level jobs in fields you find interesting – law and accounting firms, small businesses, insurance agencies, bakeries, whatever. Engage in mind-expanding activities, such as clubs and organizations. You can even attend college classes without matriculating. It's called *auditing*; no exams are required, there are no papers to write, and you pay far less than a fellow student who's enrolled in a degree program. You can also read the textbooks professors prescribe, gaining most of the knowledge you seek but incurring little to no cost. This "try before you buy" approach is a great way to test your notion that a given major is right for you.

2. They haven't considered the type of employer they'd like to work for

It's not enough to enter a college knowing what career you want to enter. You must also know what kind of employer you want to work for.

Employers fall into three major groups:

a. **For-profit companies.** These range from small, family-owned businesses that employ just a few people to the biggest, best-known corporations in America that employ hundreds of thousands of people. Big or small, these companies all have the same goal: to make money. And they all do this by earning a profit, by getting their stock price to rise – or by doing both. The best companies succeed by delivering a great customer experience while selling valued products or services at competitive prices. The *private sector* (as this group is called) employs 135 million people, or about 70% of the country's workforce, according to the Bureau of Labor Statistics. About half of private-sector workers are at large, publicly traded companies; the other half work for privately owned enterprises.

b. **The government (known as the *public sector* since all the money it spends is provided by taxpayers and lenders).** Departments and agencies of federal, state and local governments employ 25 million people. Five million of them (including two million in the military) work for the federal government (which is, by the way, the largest employer in the country). Five million work for state governments and the rest (15 million people) work for local governments.[1]

c. **Non-profit organizations.** Charities, foundations and other groups serve the community and the people living in it. Sometimes the "community" is the entire country (as in the case of the American Red Cross); for other groups, the community is a neighborhood (picture a food bank that feeds the homeless). These organizations usually give away (rather than sell) their products or services, so the money they receive generally comes from donations from governments, businesses, other non-profits and individuals. Non-profits are constantly seeking such financial support; without it, they can't remain in operation.

Generally, salaries are highest and benefits most generous in the private sector. It operates as a *meritocracy*, meaning compensation (and even your ability to keep your job) is largely based on your performance. Two people in the same job at the same employer might have sharply different incomes because one outperforms the other. Benefits are also usually generous, because companies are competing for the most talented workers. Productivity is a very high concern for companies, so they'd rather pay you a lot of money than give you a lot of time off.

---

[1] Nearly one million teachers work in the nation's schools, making it the most common occupation in state and local governments. Can you guess the second most common occupation? The answer: prison guard.

Salaries are more modest in the public sector; everyone in a given job there gets the same compensation (often adjusted for tenure and sometimes based on the level of education you've obtained). Bonuses or salary raises for a job well done are rare to non-existent; a great schoolteacher earns pretty much the same compensation as a terrible one. But benefits are often generous, partly because productivity isn't a priority. And since salaries are limited, there's often extensive benefits (teachers get summers off, for example).

Non-profits tend to pay the least because of their limited resources (although the largest offer more competitive compensation packages), so they try to offer benefits (such as a lot of vacation time) that don't require a cash outlay. As with governments, productivity isn't the goal; serving the community is. People who work for non-profits and governments often refer to a calling rather than a career; they regard their lower compensation as part of their commitment to their cause.

Each of the three groups of employers is a valuable element of our society. Choosing which to work for is not a right or wrong decision; it's just a preference. Many people start with one and move to another during their working lives. So, try to decide which of these groups currently appeals to you the most for now; you can always switch later.

And the only way you make the right choice is to talk with people who are doing what you hope to do. Want to be a doctor? Then, talk to doctors. Talk to some who are officers in the U.S. Army, others who work for the local hospital and those who operate their own medical practice.

Want to work as a schoolteacher? Graphic designer? Physical therapist? Whatever you want to do, go talk to the people who are already doing it. Ask them about their career path – and about salaries.[2] And remember to ask about benefits, since they can be 50% of your total compensation. (You'll discover that employers often get creative with their benefit packages. Supermarkets, clothing retailers and hotel chains often give employees discounts on the products they sell.)[3]

I said there are three kinds of employers. Actually, there's a fourth potential employer: yourself. Don't ignore the idea of entrepreneurship. More than 10% of the workforce, or 17 million people, are self-employed. As I'm one of the most successful entrepreneurs and business owners in the country, it's naturally a choice I endorse. So let me give you some thoughts on the topic to help you decide whether you ought to go to college if you're planning to start your own business.

The Good News About Entrepreneurship

There are lots of benefits to being self-employed. Among them:

- **Flexibility and freedom.** You get to set your own schedule. You decide when, where and how you work, and even who to accept as employees and customers. All this can help you achieve a better work-life balance.

---

[2] Don't be rude by asking "How much money do you make?" Ask instead, "Generally speaking, what is the salary range for people in this field?" You can also find this information online quite easily.

[3] Hesitant to ask folks? Try it anyway. You'll be pleasantly surprised with the warm and helpful response you'll get (most of the time, anyway). People in the midst of their careers love to help students with their career aspirations. Just be respectful and polite, and you'll soon learn how to emulate the professional responses you receive – and how to avoid repeating the poor behavior you might occasionally encounter.

- **Pursuing your passion.** Being self-employed means you get to choose your field. Don't like some duties? You get to delegate them so you can focus on doing what you love. Self-employed people like to brag about their job satisfaction compared to those who work for others.
- **Control over business decisions.** You're the boss, so you get to make all the decisions. That autonomy can be empowering and lead to a more fulfilling career.
- **Unlimited earning potential.** Unlike a job where compensation is usually limited, building your own company gives you the opportunity to make as much money as you want. The harder you work and the luckier you are (by being in the right place at the right time with the right solution and the awareness and willingness to capitalize on the moment), the greater your financial reward.
- **Tax benefits.** Self-employed people incur lots of expenses – including a home office, travel costs, business-related purchases and so on. You get to reduce the amount you pay in federal and state income taxes because of the business expenses you incur.
- **Increased retirement savings.** The law lets self-employed people contribute far more to their retirement savings accounts than people who work for others. This not only further reduces your annual income taxes, it also dramatically increases the amount of wealth you'll have in the future, compared to employed people.

The Bad News About Entrepreneurship

But there are lots of downsides to being self-employed, too. These include:

- **Frightful financials.** People with office jobs need to give no thought to how their desk, chair, phone and photocopier got there. Hospital personnel merely use their facility's tools and equipment with no notion of the cost or effort in procuring them. But that's not true for self-employed people. As the business owner, everything is entirely up to you. If you don't make it happen, it doesn't happen. This leads to a frightening financial experience for all new business start-ups, including:
  - *Immediate and ongoing business expenses.* You start spending money the day you start your business, long before you start generating any income. You'll need money to get started, but where will it come from?
  - *Income instability.* Unlike a job that provides a consistent income, your life as a newly self-employed person is filled with financial uncertainty. It could be months before you land a client or make a sale, and a couple more months before you get paid for the work you've done. How will you pay your bills in the meantime?
  - *No employee benefits.* Employers give their workers generous benefits. But you get none of those. If you get sick and can't work, not only are you not earning money that day, you must pay your own medical bills. And you can forget about vacations, because you won't be able to afford to take

14 days off without earning an income. (My wife and I took our first vacation 10 years after starting our company. It was another four years before we took another one.)

Quite frankly, there aren't many people who can handle the stress of not knowing how much income they might earn or when it might start. Even if you can handle the uncertainty or variability, that doesn't mean your spouse or kids can.

- **The owner is also the janitor.** Operating your own business means you must handle everything. That has two downsides:
  - *You must be an expert in everything.* You're starting a business because you're passionate about something – and you're probably an *SME*, a subject-matter expert in that field. But it's not enough that self-employed graphic designers know all about Photoshop; they must also know all about:
    - Legal and compliance
      - How to structure your business (sole proprietorship, C-Corp, S-Corp, LLC, etc.)
      - Understanding contracts and agreements
      - Intellectual property rights (trademarks, copyrights, patents)
      - Business licenses and regulatory requirements
      - Client dispute resolution
    - Finance and accounting
      - Budgeting and managing cash flow
      - Invoicing, bookkeeping and financial tracking
      - Understanding self-employment taxes
      - Pricing your products or services correctly
      - Securing business loans or funding

- Branding and marketing
  - Creating a strong brand identity
  - Digital marketing (search engine optimization, social media, email marketing)
  - Content creation and storytelling
  - Networking and building a professional reputation
- Sales and negotiation
  - How to sell your products or services effectively
  - Understanding customer needs and pain points
  - Contract negotiation and closing deals
  - Building customer loyalty and retention
- Customer service and relationship management
  - Handling client expectations professionally
  - Dealing with difficult customers
  - Building long-term customer relationships
- Technology and digital tools
  - Using accounting software
  - Website development and maintenance
  - Cybersecurity to protect business data
- Business management
  - Goal setting and strategic planning
  - Managing growth and scaling your business
- Productivity and time management
  - Setting and staying focused on priorities
  - Using productivity tools
  - Balancing work-life responsibilities
- Self-motivation and resilience
  - Staying disciplined without a boss

- Overcoming setbacks and failures
- Maintaining motivation during slow periods
- *So much for passion.* You started your business because you have a passion for something, but instead you're finding yourself spending most of your time engaged in all the activities listed here. Considering all these obligations, when exactly is the baker supposed to find the time to bake?
- **There's no work-life balance for the entrepreneur.** I've never met a successful business owner who works part-time. It's exactly the opposite: Entrepreneurs tend to work 60 to 80 hours per week. I know I did: 12 hours a day, six days a week, plus four hours on Sundays. Total: 76 hours a week. Some people admired my success and have told me how smart I am, but quite frankly, being smart had little to do with it. I simply worked harder. When asked how I was able to grow my firm faster than everyone else, I explained that it was simply because I worked 24 months per year. You see, most people work 40 hours a week for 50 weeks a year (the other two weeks are used for vacation and sick leave). That's 2,000 hours of work per year. But I was working 3,952 hours annually, or twice as much. So, what they accomplished in two years I was able to do in just one year.[4] Sure, I used my skills and made some smart decisions, but quite frankly, if I hadn't worked so hard, those skills and decisions would not have mattered much.

---

[4] Remember when I said I got my degree in 3½ years?

Sure, you can work part-time, like an Uber driver, but that's a gig and an entirely different conversation. It's not entrepreneurship in the context of this discussion.[5]

If you think my working so many hours was dumb, then get a job. Entrepreneurship isn't for you. And that's OK; only 10% of workers choose the entrepreneurial path.

While self-employment can be incredibly rewarding – and I am here as testament to all it offers – that path is not without its challenges. You'll need discipline, resilience, willingness to sacrifice and ability to adapt to the unpredictable.

If your path is indeed self-employment, you have one major question to answer at this time: Should you get a college degree? Here are five reasons yes, and two reasons no:

Five Reasons Budding Entrepreneurs Should First Get a College Degree

1. **You'll gain vital business and financial knowledge.** You've seen the skill set needed to succeed in operating a business; college courses give you that content.
2. **Networking opportunities.** College connects you with professors, peers and alumni who could become your future business partners, mentors and customers. The relationships you'll build will be invaluable to your efforts to start and operate a successful business.

---

[5] And yes, I'm a big fan of gigs. You ought to have several of them. Read my book, *The Truth About Your Future,* for more on this.

3. **Credibility.** Promoting your degree can add credibility when meeting with potential investors, lenders, customers and employees.
4. **Discipline, time management and organizational skills.** College teaches you many of the skills that are essential in operating your business.
5. **Backup.** If your enterprise fails, having a degree can improve your ability to get hired by someone.

Two Reasons to Skip College If Self-Employment Is Your Future

1. **No degree required.** Depending on your field, real-world experience could be more practical and valuable than the time and money you'd spend getting a college degree. Plus, you get to start now, instead of maybe six years from now. You'll learn from trial and error – and your failures along the way will provide priceless practical experience. And even though you're not going to college, you can still get much of the education through books and online platforms like Udemy, Coursera and YouTube. Every successful business owner I know reads lots of business books, surfs the web and goes to lots of business conferences that offer seminars and continuing education programs. No degree required.

2. **Spend the money on your business instead of college.** You've seen how hard it is to get a college degree and how often people fail in their attempt to graduate. If you plan to be self-employed, investing that time and money into building your business may be the smarter financial move.

If you do choose the college route, take courses that will directly benefit your self-employed career. These include:

- *Business Administration:* This provides you the education you need about entrepreneurship, business management and finance.
- *Branding, Marketing, Social Media, Graphic Design and Content Creation:* All these are essential for building a successful enterprise.
- *Accounting, Finance and Economics:* These teach you how to manage business expenses, taxes and budgets, and give you an understanding of how the capital markets operate (vital, since that's the world you'll be entering as a business owner).
- *Communication and Public Speaking:* These improve your negotiation, sales and networking skills.
- *Sociology, Psychology and History:* Understanding what motivates individuals and societies will help you craft your business strategies.

Ideally, choose a college or university that offers a degree in entrepreneurship, with classes taught by professors who are former business owners and entrepreneurs themselves. (Don't be overly impressed by retired corporate executives – that career path is very different from that of would-be business start-ups like you.)

3. They get a college degree to enter a field that doesn't require one

Being a mail sorter with the U.S. Postal Service is a fine occupation. The average salary is $36,838, according to Salary.com, and there are ample benefits, including a *pension* (monthly payments you receive for life if you retire after working for USPS for at least 20 years; the average benefit is about $1,000, says USPS). Even better, USPS doesn't require mail sorters to have a college degree.

And yet, 37% of them do!

This is not an isolated example. As Table 10.1 shows, millions of people have a college degree but are working in occupations that don't require one. And every one of these jobs pays 50% to 100% more than the national average of $48,000, according to the Bureau of Labor Statistics.

I'm not saying you should skip college to go work in one of these jobs. But I am saying this: For whatever field you plan to enter, investigate whether a college degree is required. If it isn't, save yourself

Table 10.1 Occupations That Don't Require a College Degree

Occupation That Doesn't Require a College Degree	Percentage of Workers with a College Degree	Average Annual Salary
Construction Managers	53%	$108,210
Insurance Agents	48%	79,700
Claims Adjusters, Examiners and Investigators	48%	72,500
Administrative Services Managers	48%	122,090
Computer User Support Specialists	39%	60,620
Transportation, Storage and Distribution Managers	38%	105,580
Police and Sheriff's Patrol Officers	30%	70,000
Real Estate Brokers and Agents	28%	68,790
Food Service Managers	24%	63,970

six years and hundreds of thousands of dollars, and go enter that field immediately upon leaving high school.

By the way, many occupations (not just the nine shown earlier) offer higher-than-average incomes with no degree required. Table 10.2 provides a bigger list for you, compliments of the BLS.

Table 10.2 Occupations Offering Higher-Than-Average Salaries, No Degree Required

Occupation	Average Salary
Nuclear Power Reactor Operators	$100,000
Power Distributors and Dispatchers	100,000
Power Plant Operators	75,000
Chemical Plant and System Operators	75,000
Gas Plant Operators	75,000
Petroleum Pump System and Refinery Operators	75,000
Transportation, Storage and Distribution Managers	105,580
Elevator and Escalator Installers and Repairers	97,860
Detectives and Criminal Investigators	83,640
Commercial Pilots	99,640
First-Line Supervisors of Police and Detectives	98,760
Electrical Power-Line Installers and Repairers	78,310
Farmers, Ranchers and Other Agricultural Managers	73,060
Plumbers, Pipefitters, and Steamfitters	59,880
Electricians	60,040
Hearing Aid Specialists	59,500
Fire Inspectors and Investigators	64,600
Claims Adjusters, Examiners and Investigators	72,500
Insurance Sales Agents	79,700
Real Estate Brokers and Sales Agents	68,790
First-Line Supervisors of Non-retail Sales Workers	84,170
First-Line Supervisors of Construction Workers	74,600

4. Or, they get a required degree, but they don't get the skills they need to succeed in that field

I mentioned in Chapter 7 that you'll be awarded a degree even if you get nothing but Cs in every class. But low grades suggest you probably haven't mastered the content that was taught.

That's why you must graduate on the dean's list – *cum laude, magna cum laude* or *summa cum laude* (with honors, with high honors or with highest honors). In fact, there are two reasons you need to achieve one of these accolades.

First, as I mentioned, having scored As in all your classes means you really know your stuff – making it far more likely that you'll be able to perform well in your new job and thus keep it.

Second, it will help you get that job in the first place. When you graduate, you'll be competing for jobs with everyone else who has recently graduated with that degree. The best way to quickly demonstrate to employers that you're worthy of consideration is to show that you are better than the other job candidates – and highlighting your dean's list ranking does precisely that.

So, you must graduate with honors.

Does that notion frighten you a bit? Achieving all As and Bs might be an intimidating goal. After all, only the smartest students get on the dean's list, right?

Wrong. It has little to do with how smart you are. It is mostly about how hard you work. And I proved it.

When I went to college, I was a terrible student at first. In the fall semester of my freshman year, my Grade Point Average was a meager 2.8, or about a C-plus. So what, I figured; I was making new friends and having a good time. In the spring semester, my fun factor rose, but my grades fell: I got a 2.4 GPA.

My sophomore year's fall semester was even worse: my GPA fell to 2.1. At this rate, I'd soon fail out of school. (I remember skipping so many math classes that when I finally did show up, I walked into an exam I knew nothing about. Obviously, I failed the course.)[6]

When grades came out and everyone excitedly talked about their GPAs, I began to realize that everyone was earning far better grades than me. Well, that's just because they all have so much time to study, I decided. I'm a busy guy! After all, I was president of the sophomore class and heavily involved in student government activities. Who's got time to study?

That was my rationale for such poor grades. But then a friend told me she'd gotten a 4.0 GPA that semester – straight As. And she was editor-in-chief of the school newspaper! We'd had friendly arguments over whose job was more difficult and took more time, but secretly I knew that hers did (because of those weekly publication deadlines). But despite her workload, she managed to get a 4.0 while I got a measly 2.1 as class president!

I was not only embarrassed with myself, I was also furious. She's not smarter than me, I silently said. If she can get a 4.0, then I can, too.

---

[6] Not only did I have to retake the course – a waste of my time – I forced my parents to pay a second time for the cost of the class. My lack of consideration for their money was selfish and rude.

And besides, I began to realize that I'm not here at college solely to have a great time and party with my friends. I'm here to learn something.

So, I decided to change my attitude. I decided that my professors weren't imparting useless information but essential knowledge that would enable me to succeed in my future career and life. Thus, I made a mental shift, a reset of my mindset.

When the spring semester began, I attended every class. But I knew that wouldn't be enough – I'm not one of those geniuses with photographic memories who can nail any exam without studying or even reading a textbook.[7]

I knew that doing well academically would take a lot of hard work to make up for the lack of brilliance that my parents lamented I didn't have. And I succeeded: That spring, I scored a 3.6 GPA (four As and a B), and in every semester afterward (my entire junior and senior years) I earned 4.0 GPAs. And I did this while serving as the Student Government Association's executive VP (the number-two position) and interning for a member of Congress.

Like I said, it was all the result of effort, not intellectual genius. So, let me share with you how I did it – because you can do it, too.

How to Score a 4.0 GPA – and Actually Learn Something

First, I took extensive notes in every class. My professors could talk faster than I could write, so I taught myself how to quickly record

---

[7] We all know kids like that, and admit it, we all hate them.

their key points. My goal was to memorialize the vital information and not get left behind as they moved on with their lectures.

I also read every chapter they assigned from the textbooks. Then, I'd read those chapters again, this time using a yellow marker to highlight all the important passages.

Next, I'd write in a notebook everything I had highlighted.

Fourth, I'd yellow-highlight the notes I'd written and, fifth, I'd summarize on 3x5 index cards all my notes from the lectures and the textbook – with each card containing one item, concept or fact.

By the time I finished, I'd have read my class notes and the textbook a total of five times, and I'd transferred the key information onto a slim set of notecards. By doing all this, I'd distilled the entire course and textbook to the core facts.

Then, the night before the exam, I'd memorize all the information on those cards.

The final step of my process was the most important. Professors didn't let us bring any materials into the exam room (except for open-book exams, of course) to prevent students from cheating. But they did provide us with a pencil and a blank sheet of paper.

So, immediately upon arrival, I wrote on that sheet everything I'd memorized from the 3x5 cards – every key fact, figure, formula and statistic. By doing so, I didn't have to keep that information in my head. Thus, I could simply refer to my notes as I read each question.

This helped me stay calm and focused during the exam, because I knew I wouldn't become overwhelmed by trying to remember everything at once. Not only did this let me answer every question correctly, I did so with amazing speed – finishing each exam far faster than other students and with no stress or sweat.

That's how I aced every test, and that's how you can, too.

To engage successfully with my process, keep one important point in mind: I did everything manually. I had no choice, because electronics didn't exist when I attended college in the 1970s (I graduated in 1980). Forget about the Internet; we didn't even have fax machines or photocopiers; we used mimeograph machines, carbon paper and Wite Out.[8]

So, I had to take all my notes with a pen and paper. Today, of course, you could execute all my steps using digital technology – your smartphone and ChatGPT can record lectures and provide summaries and you can get textbook summaries online.

Don't do that.

Instead, stick with pen and paper. I'm not saying this because I'm an old fart. I'm saying this because you'll get better results. Studies in 2025 proved that using pen and paper improves recall and comprehension compared to the use of electronic devices.

You see, when you type on a keyboard, every muscle action is the same. Press the letters *r* and *q*. You'll see there's no difference in movement. But when you write *r*, your hand's motion is very different from writing *q*. That physical movement helps your brain process the content. Also, since you can't write as fast as you can type, writing by hand forces you to move more slowly – and by going slower, you naturally focus more on what you're writing.

Too often, students typing notes in class simply quote verbatim from lectures. That's merely acting as a stenographer; there's no comprehension. But when you write notes with a pen, you have to

---

[8] Google it.

summarize what the professor says – and this forces you to analyze and interpret what you hear. The result: You'll write less but comprehend more.

In other words, typing does not engage your brain as much as writing does. And engagement is the key. Technology and automation might be efficient, but they are not as effective in helping you become a subject-matter expert.

Scientists actually have a name for this. It's called *cognitive offloading* – meaning typing on a keyboard doesn't get the content into your brain; instead, it merely goes into the cloud or a hard drive. Writing by hand, by contrast, engages the parts of your brain that help you learn – preventing the offloading that typing facilitates. This was also confirmed by a 2024 study that found higher levels of electrical activity in the brains of college students who took notes by hand compared to those who typed their notes.

Yes, I know textbooks are expensive and that you can save money by downloading a summary. Buy and read the book, anyway. There are no shortcuts to learning and gaining knowledge. If you can't afford to buy the books, then you can't afford to go to college. It's that simple.

I'm sure you understand what I'm saying, because this is really quite simple. But it's not easy to do. I found that I was spending twice as much time studying outside class as I was spending time in class. In other words, a semester filled with five classes, each 75 minutes held twice a week, is 12.5 hours of class time per week. And that meant I was studying another 25 hours per week – a total of 37.5 hours. That's a full-time job! (That explains why I don't recommend that you work part-time while in school.)

You might get pushback from roommates (I did) who urge you to close the textbooks and party with them. If you encounter those pressures, you need new roommates and friends. You're not spending massive amounts of money attending college so you can major in partying. You're not going to college primarily to have fun. You're there to learn so you can develop the knowledge and skills that let you embark on a rewarding and successful career.

> I shouldn't have to mention this, but the statistics show that I do. So here goes.
>
> It's bad enough that students type their notes instead of handwriting them. But far worse is delegating it all to AI.
>
> A 2023 survey from Study.com found that 9 in 10 college students (89%) are using AI chatbots to read their assigned work for them, complete their homework and/or write their papers.
>
> This is cheating. Period.
>
> Worse, it's stupid. Or rather, such cheating will keep you stupid. A 2025 study by researchers at MIT found that 83% of students who used AI to help them write papers had difficulty quoting from their submissions. In other words, they knew no more after completing their assignments than they had before they started.

Using AI to take your quiz or write your paper might score you an A while alleviating yourself of the time and burden of doing the work yourself, but the result is that you'll know nothing more at the end of the semester than you did before you started it. You'll merely be six months older and thousands of dollars poorer.

And while such cheating might trick your professor into giving you an A, good luck trying to get an employer to give you (or let you keep) a job after it quickly becomes clear that you have no idea how to do the job you supposedly went to college to learn how to do.

It's not just students who are cheating. So are college professors. Consulting group Tyton Partners surveyed thousands of faculty members and found that more than a third (36%) are using AI to create courses, write exam questions, evaluate student papers – and even engage in online chats so the human profs don't have to.

Add this to your list of questions (coming later in this chapter) when you evaluate colleges. Ask about the school's policy governing faculty use of AI.

---

5. They don't know that the field they're pursuing doesn't offer many jobs

A friend said his daughter loves Walmart, and she's studying business management so she can one day manage a Walmart store, where managers earn up to $620,000 a year.

Two big mistakes here. First, she apparently didn't bother asking if Walmart requires its store managers to hold a college degree (it doesn't, and they don't; 75% of Walmart store managers began their careers in hourly jobs). Knowing this should compel her to drop out of school (saving all the time and money of pursuing a degree) and get a job at Walmart as a cashier or clerk, to begin her way up the career ladder.

Second, she also failed to consider that there are only 4,600 Walmart stores in the United States – and thus only 4,600 store managers. And all those jobs are filled – meaning she'll have to wait for one of those managers to get fired, quit, retire, become disabled or die. And even when there's an opening, she'll be competing with every other Walmart employee who wants to be a store manager.

And how many people will she be competing with? Lots! Walmart is the country's largest corporate employer, with more than 1.6 million workers. Is she being realistic believing she will be selected one day as a Walmart store manager?

OK, so maybe that story isn't resonating with you because you're not interested in being a Walmart store manager. How about becoming a sociologist? Sociology is the twenty-fifth most popular major among college students; every year, 329 institutions give 35,800 people a degree in sociology, according to College Factual. Yet, only 3,300 people work as sociologists, according to the Bureau of Labor Statistics. Every year, we're issuing 10 times more sociology degrees than there are such jobs!

I once chatted with a professor of sociology at a school where tuition is more than $30,000 per year. Had he told his students that there are few jobs in that field and that everyone working in the field needs a graduate degree? He said he hadn't.

"My job is to teach them sociology," he said.

"No," I replied, "Your job is to prepare your students to live successful, happy lives. And having them spend six years and $150,000 on a degree without giving them this information is irresponsible."

He shrugged.

Two related thoughts. First, an Axios/Generation Lab survey found that 16% of college students want to work for Google when they graduate. What a fine aspiration.

But there's a problem: About four million people graduate from college each year, meaning 640,000 of them want to work for Google. Yet the company had only 2,463 job listings in February 2025, according to Glassdoor. In other words, only 0.004% of those wanting a job at Google can actually get one. The other 99.996% will fail.

Second, college students surveyed by Real Estate Witch said they expect to earn, on average, $85,000 in their first job and more than $200,000 after 10 years. Yet, the average starting salary for college graduates is $55,000, or 35% less. And the actual mid-career salary for graduates is $98,000, or just half of what college students expect to earn 10 years after graduation.

Before you spend the next four years and massive amounts of money to obtain a college degree, do a little research to see if you can truly get a job in the field you're seeking to enter, and at the level of compensation you want, to justify the investment you're about to make.

Be certain of this fact: It is *guaranteed* that you will undergo this investigation. Either you will be smart and do it while you're in high school or you'll do it *after* you're a college graduate. Too often, it's only after someone has a degree and is seeking a job that they discover whether the job they'd envisioned actually exists and is attainable.

One additional point: Your challenge in finding employment in your chosen field is made even more difficult if the field you've selected is filled with what economists call *zero-sum* jobs.

Let me explain. If you want to be a chef, you'll find virtually unlimited opportunities available, because chefs are needed by so many employers – from restaurants to caterers to wealthy families. But if you want to be the lead actor in a Broadway play, the only way for you to get the job is for someone else to lose it. That is the zero-sum scenario: Only one person can succeed at a time. As in poker, I can't win unless you lose.

A more pleasant outcome is when both people seeking a job can succeed in getting one. Every physician can be hired as a doctor. Every singer can get signed as a recording artist. But only 32 people can be first-string quarterbacks in the National Football League. That means 12,946 of the 12,978 starting quarterbacks on high school football teams will fail to get that job in the NFL. Most won't try, but thousands will – and only 0.003% of high school quarterbacks will succeed. I hope those 12,946 players have a backup plan.

Don't set yourself on an unrealistic path. I wonder: How many college graduates are sorting mail at the post office today because they weren't realistic about all this?

> Whoa.
>
> I don't want you to leave this section thinking I hate the liberal arts and that the only path to career success lies with STEM degrees (science, technology, engineering and math).
>
> Keep in mind that my wife Jean and I were both liberal arts majors (communications with a minor in public relations for me; nutrition and consumer economics for Jean). Yeah, our decisions were 50+ years ago, but consider this: Far more recently, my wife and I became the benefactors of Rowan University's Ric Edelman College of Communication, Humanities & Social Sciences. Why would we do that – and why would we have endowed the school with $10 million to fund Edelman Scholars (undergraduate students who receive both a completely free college education plus $17,500 in cash if they graduate in four years on the dean's list)?
>
> Obviously, we believe today in the value of a liberal arts education just as much as we did half a century ago.
>
> *(Continued)*

(Continued)

For years, high school students have been urged to pursue STEM degrees – and so far in the book, you too might have gotten that sense (however unintentionally on my part) – based on the promise of job readiness, higher salaries and future-proof careers.

But a deeper look at employment trends, salary trajectories and the rise of AI suggests that this so-called wisdom is flawed. The truth is that students who major in the humanities and liberal arts may actually be better positioned not only to thrive in today's dynamic economy but also to lead it.

Although STEM graduates often begin their careers with higher starting salaries, those with humanities and social sciences degrees frequently surpass them by mid-career. In 2019, Harvard economist David Deming reported that, by age 40, graduates in social sciences and history earn on average $131,154, compared to $124,458 for those in computer science and engineering. That research was later supported by the Federal Reserve Bank of New York, using 2023 Census Data, which found that unemployment rates among recent graduates in STEM fields have been higher than for those in many humanities fields. For example, computer science and computer engineering grads had unemployment rates of 6.1% and 7.5%, respectively, while the unemployment rate for art history majors was 3% and only 0.4% for nutrition majors. Clearly, these data challenge the assumption that STEM is synonymous with job security.

Even for those managing to be employed, salaries aren't always higher for the STEM degree holders. Bankrate in 2023 found that while STEM majors often start their careers with significantly higher salaries than humanities majors, the earnings gap narrows over time. Political science grads, for example, start out earning an average of $54,000, but that later rises to $90,000 – comparable to chemistry majors. Table 10.3 shows Payscale.com data of average salaries in 2024 of those who graduated 10 years ago.

Why do liberal arts majors do so well in a tech-focused economy? Because their careers often shift toward management, law, business and leadership roles where critical thinking and communication matter more than technical expertise. By contrast, a student trained as a computer coder can only code – a career-liming skill set.

This is demonstrated by the fact that within a year of graduation, 30% of STEM graduates are underemployed or working outside their field. The issue isn't a shortage of STEM jobs; it's skills misalignment. Employers today aren't just looking for coders or analysts. They want employees who can think critically, communicate clearly and adapt quickly – skills humanities majors develop in abundance.

(Continued)

(Continued)

Table 10.3 Salaries 10 Years After Graduation

Economics	$130,200
Civil Engineering	$122,600
Political Science	$106,200
Philosophy	$105,500
Accounting	$105,100
Occupational Therapy	$103,200
International Studies	$ 98,500
English	$ 97,100
Business Administration	$ 96,300
Biology	$ 93,600
History	$ 93,400
Public Relations	$ 93,000
Spanish	$ 88,800
Psychology	$ 83,400
Anthropology	$ 82,100
Sociology	$ 81,800
Africana Studies	$ 76,100
Speech Pathology	$ 74,600
Clinical Psychology	$ 74,300
Health and Exercise Science	$ 72,600

Indeed, the 2025 Job Outlook published by the National Association of Colleges and Employers says:

- 90% of recruiters prioritize problem-solving.
- 80% seek teamwork and collaboration.
- More than 70% value written communication, initiative and adaptability.

These are not technical skills; they are human skills – the kind cultivated through a liberal arts education.

The World Economic Forum's *Future of Jobs* report said the same thing, noting that the top in-demand skills for the future workforce include analytical thinking, innovation and adaptability. Only two of the top seven future skills cited are technical.

If you want to master the marketplace in our growing age of automation, you want to develop strategic and essential capabilities in collaboration, emotional intelligence, ethical reasoning and cultural awareness. For sure, one study that analyzed 70 million job transitions and 20 million résumés found that foundational human skills like communication and critical thinking are key attributes that enable professionals to move up the career ladder.

Contrary to the myth that humanities degrees are "too broad and general," these programs offer deep

(Continued)

(Continued)
specialization. For instance, history includes public historians, labor historians and digital archivists. Sociology offers tracks in health, urban and international sociology. Political science graduates work in governance, policy and global relations.

And it might be counterintuitive, but AI is making a degree in the humanities more essential than ever. AI excels at pattern recognition, but it lacks context, ethical reasoning and original thought. It cannot judge what *should* be done – only what *can* be done.

So as we build increasingly complex AI systems, there's a growing recognition that humanities-trained professionals are essential in shaping these technologies. Ethicists, cultural theorists and philosophers are increasingly working on AI development teams. That's because responsible technology development requires design and governance guidance, inclusivity and fairness and a focus on connecting innovation to public understanding.

Indeed, a 2025 article published by the Institute of Electrical and Electronics Engineers argued for the integration of social sciences and humanities into AI development as core partners with decision-making power. The ability to ask tough questions – Is this ethical? Who does this benefit? What are the long-term societal impacts? – requires a human touch grounded in historical, philosophical and social understanding.

And liberal arts majors aren't succeeding in the workplace merely as participants. They are also succeeding by leading. To wit:

- 60% of American CEOs have humanities backgrounds.
- A third of Fortune 500 CEOs majored in the humanities.
- More than half of U.S. governors hold degrees in the humanities or social sciences.

This is proof that a liberal arts education equips people to lead, regardless of industry.

This is why Jean and I agreed to underwrite the Ric Edelman College of Communication, Humanities & Social Sciences at Rowan University. We're helping to redefine what a liberal arts education means in the twenty-first century; far from being outdated and undesirable in today's job market, the college's programs are interdisciplinary, experiential and directly aligned with today's real-world demands.

At the Ric Edelman College, students get the critical thinking, ethical leadership and adaptability skills they need – especially in today's era that's being shaped by AI and automation. The Ric Edelman College is perhaps the only liberal arts program in the country that requires students to complete an Experiential Learning project, such as our collaboration with NASA on future disaster response plans in space.

(Continued)

(Continued)

The college also features:

- **The Center for Professional Success**, which secures internships (offering up to 12 credits), networking, travel funding and workshops.
- **Centers and institutes**, such as the Center for the Advancement of Women in Communication Writing, that provide students with hands-on learning in ethics, policy, anthropology and more.
- **New degrees** in digital humanities, emergency management, cannabis policy, African American history and blockchain applications to assure students they're ready to work in emerging fields.
- **The 3+3 Law Program** that lets students earn both a bachelor's and JD degree in just six years, letting graduates enter the workforce a year faster while saving tens of thousands of dollars.

And rather than being too general, the Ric Edelman College offers students deep specialization in such fields as:

- Digital historians
- Health sociologists
- Ethicists in AI
- Digital humanities
- Emergency management
- Holocaust and genocide education
- African American History Education certificate

- Cannabis policy and studies
- Blockchain applications in business and social sciences

Throughout all these programs, students are taught civic responsibility, cultural and historical awareness, ethical reasoning, critical thinking, imagination and creativity – which helps them establish lifelong intellectual curiosity.

This is no outdated set of coursework, and there's little resemblance to the liberal arts degree I got at Rowan in 1980 (back then, known as Glassboro State College). Today's degree from the Ric Edelman College gives students rigorous, practical and relevant education that blends critical inquiry with real-world action, with the primary goal of preparing students to get jobs. This is a new model for higher education, and we're proud to support it. Sure, studying tech sounds state-of-the-art, but all this sounds pretty cool, too.

So, don't think a sociology degree is necessarily a waste of time and money – even though it's highly unlikely that you'd end up working as a sociologist. What you'll get is career agility that helps you adapt, lead and learn over an entire lifetime. It will teach you to think ethically and critically in this new era of rapid change.

We're all facing domination by data and automation, and that means the value of being human has never been higher. That's why the smartest career path in the twenty-first century just might be the liberal arts.

6. They fail to realize they've chosen a field that requires a postgraduate degree or professional certification

Not a single one of those 35,800 sociology majors will get a job as a sociologist if all they end up with is a bachelor's degree. That's because sociologists must have at least a master's degree, and often a doctorate, to work in the field. How many of those 35,800 graduates knew that when they selected sociology as their major?

A degree in biology doesn't entitle you to become a physician. You'll also need to graduate from medical school and, for many specialties, become board-certified.

Law school graduates must pass the bar exam before they can practice law. Accounting majors must pass the CPA exam. Those with education degrees must obtain state certificates to teach schoolchildren.

In dozens of fields, a bachelor's degree is merely the first step. This means you might need to complete far more than four years of college. In most states, CPA candidates must complete five years of undergraduate study and then pass four exams over two years; lawyers must complete three years of law school and pass the bar exam; physicians complete as many as six years of additional education, plus pass board exams. And for many fields, a PhD is required; dissertations can take decades to complete. (In college you hear of

ABDs – people who have nearly completed their schooling as they have accomplished "all but dissertation.")

In addition to the extra time you'll need to complete all this education, you're going to spend a ton more money. The average cost of law school is $230,000, says the Education Data Initiative. Medical school costs an average of $238,000, and an MBA takes $60,000 to $200,000 and two years.

Here's the key fact: Only 17% of college graduates go on to graduate school, but they owe most of the student debt. Indeed, EDI says undergrads owe an average of $30,000, while those who went to graduate school owe an average of $103,000.

So, if your chosen career requires you to complete graduate, law or medical school, it's even more important that you minimize your student debt as an undergrad. Simultaneously, anticipate right now, from the very beginning of your college journey, the total cost in time, money and effort of what you're planning to pursue. Because if you don't realize what it's going to take until you're in the midst of it, you may well quit once you realize how hard it is. And remember, whatever money you'd spent is gone and any loans you took must still be repaid.

7. They obtain a graduate degree without regard to ROI

You're probably assuming that those with graduate degrees are better off financially than those who merely hold a bachelor's degree. That assumption is wrong.

A 2024 study by the Foundation for Research on Equal Opportunity found that 43% of master's degree programs lead to negative ROI. Graduate degrees cost a lot of money but produce only modest increases in earnings – a bad combination.

This is why you must consider your field and its job opportunities. You may discover that a master's degree has no economic value – or you might find a way to make that graduate degree pay off really well.

Education is a great case in point. There are 3.2 million schoolteachers in the United States, and they all have a bachelor's degree. But school systems want their teachers to be as highly trained as possible, so they encourage their faculty members to get a master's degree. This encouragement comes with an enticement: teachers who have a master's degree earn higher salaries.

No wonder 48% of the nation's schoolteachers hold a graduate degree, says National University. But were these teachers all really that smart to get those graduate degrees?

Maybe, maybe not. It depends on how much they paid for their graduate degree and how many more years they'll teach once they get it. Consider this: The average teacher with a bachelor's degree earns $66,397 per year, according to the National Education Association, while the average teacher with a master's degree in education (M.Ed.) earns an average of $73,037, or 10% more.

Yet the M.Ed. costs an average of $44,640, says Coursera, and some programs cost more than $100,000. Does it make sense to spend $44,640 to earn an extra $4,648 after taxes? Maybe, if you're going to work 15+ more years. Less than that, and you'd be better off investing that $44,640 and letting it grow. Less work, with a better financial outcome.

But there's a different answer, too. You can massively improve the ROI of that M.Ed. by sharply reducing its cost. And that's easy to do: State universities offer online master's programs for as little as $8,840! Wow – your pay increase will cover that in less than two years, and then you get to enjoy the higher income for the rest of your career! Now, that is a great deal and a fabulous ROI!

I wonder how many schoolteachers are getting their master's degrees at such low costs. I couldn't find any data on this, so I don't know. But the mere fact that programs exist at prices of $100,000 tells me that there are at least some teachers (few, I hope) who are going about this completely wrong.

So, if you're going to pursue a graduate degree, treat it as an investment decision. To do that, just answer these questions:

1. How much will the graduate degree cost?
2. How much additional income will I earn as a result of obtaining that degree?
3. Will having this degree improve my efforts to achieve happiness?

An analysis of these answers will help you determine if pursuing a graduate degree is worth the time, money and effort.

8. They don't realize that technology will eliminate the career they're planning to pursue

As I explain in my book, *The Truth About Your Future,* exponential technologies will render about half of all occupations obsolete. I'm talking about artificial intelligence and machine learning, quantum computing, robotics, nanotechnology, biotechnology and bioinformatics, 3D and 4D printing, virtual and augmented reality (the metaverse), distributed ledger technology (aka blockchain, tokenization, and digital assets, broadly referred to as crypto), FinTech, EdTech, AgTech (finance, education and agriculture technology), aviation technology, neuroscience and more. Job obsolescence is already underway and will increase over the next decade.

This notion isn't new, that technology eliminates jobs; this has occurred for hundreds of years. What's new is that innovations that used to occur over a generation now occur in mere years. It took four generations for us to get where we are: 160 years ago, most people worked on farms. Their children worked in factories, their children worked in offices and their children (you) can often work anywhere. We went from the Agricultural Age to the Industrial Age to the Information Age to . . . whatever we'll be calling the age you'll find yourself in 10 years from now.

Consider the impact of all this. In 1870, half of all workers in the United States worked on farms, according to the Bureau of Labor

Statistics and the Census Bureau. By 1950, fewer than 10% did. Today, farms employ under 1% of the nation's workers, even though the agriculture industry produces more food than ever.

Law firms are now using AI to instantly find court rulings relevant to their cases – work that used to be done by first-year associates fresh out of law school. Drones survey and map construction sites in 30 minutes; humans needed two weeks to perform those tasks. A quantum computer chip developed by Google in December 2024 completed a computation in five minutes that would take today's fastest supercomputers 525,600,000,000,000,000,000,000,000,000 minutes. That's 10 septillion years, which is more time than has existed since the creation of the universe.

These examples explain why Oxford University says nearly half of all occupations are at high risk of being taken over by exponential technologies. Most people are oblivious to what's coming; many others are in denial. When a friend told me his son is studying to become an accountant, I said that field likely won't exist by the time the lad is 35. "Nonsense," my friend said. "We'll always need accountants."

Well, we'll always need accounting, but that doesn't mean we'll always need human accountants. Accounting is little more than collecting, storing, analyzing and reporting numbers. To suggest that we'll continue to need humans to do that work is as silly as saying no one would ever prefer to use a calculator when they can instead use a pencil and paper to do multiplication and division. Tax software is already free, for example, enabling millions of taxpayers to avoid the expense of hiring a paid tax preparer. This trend will increase as technology gets better and cheaper.

If you were a business owner, would you rather use a free or low-cost AI program to track your income and expenses, or spend $200,000 per year (the average compensation of CPAs, including salary, benefits and payroll taxes, according to UWorld Accounting)? Keep in mind that AI works 24/7 and never calls in sick or takes vacation. It doesn't discriminate, get drunk during working hours, sexually harass staff (which can get your company sued) or commit fraud – all of which can and does happen with human workers. And by not having to hire a roomful of CPAs, you avoid the need to hire managers to supervise them. The cost savings are immense – which is why it is inevitable that the accounting profession will largely cease to exist in the next decade or so.

> This metamorphosis is already underway. There were 16% fewer accountants and auditors in the United States in 2024 than in 2019. In 2024, there were 1.7 million people in this field, but from 2019 to 2024, 300,000 accountants quit their jobs.
>
> At the same time, fewer college students are majoring in accounting than a decade ago. These students know that accountants earn less than stock analysts, investment bankers and financial planners. They also know that accountants must complete a fifth year of college (at a cost of maybe $50,000) and then pass the CPA exam – a test that only half pass. *Five years of college, a huge failure rate and less pay even if you do succeed? Forget it. I'm going to join a Wall Street firm instead.*

Indeed, that's not just the conclusion of lots of college students, who are majoring in business and finance instead of accounting – it's also the conclusion of those 300,000 CPAs who have left accounting for better-paying jobs as financial analysts, investment bankers and financial planners.

Will business suffer without human accountants? It doesn't seem so, because the big accounting firms are gearing up to replace humans with technology. PricewaterhouseCoopers announced plans to spend $1 billion on Generative AI while Deloitte and E&Y are each spending $1.4 billion and KPMG is spending $2 billion.

So, if you think you can fill out a tax form better than a computer, go ahead and major in accounting. But by that logic, you ought to also consider training to be an elevator operator.

This isn't just a rant against pursuing a career in accounting. AI is an existential threat to hundreds of occupations – and harming newly minted college graduates the most. In May 2025, Aneesh Raman, LinkedIn's chief economic opportunity officer, said, "Artificial intelligence poses a real threat to the entry-level jobs that normally serve as the first step for each new generation of young workers."

His point: AI can (or soon will) do the jobs that used to be done by young workers. AI can write and debug computer code (something junior programmers have been doing); it can find relevant case law (which paralegals and first-year associates traditionally did); and it can manage help desks, engaging directly with customers (which retailers once needed customer service reps for). This is a big reason why the unemployment rate for college graduates has risen 50% since 2023, according to Oxford Economics. And this is happening across majors, says Burning Glass Institute, from visual arts to engineering. Indeed, unemployment among recent college graduates is now rising faster than it is for young adults with just high-school or associate degrees, and for the first time in 45 years, people with a college degree have a higher unemployment rate than the national average.

Goldman Sachs says two-thirds of all the jobs in the United States and Europe are vulnerable to AI, and that automation might replace 300 million workers. No wonder that 30% of workers say they're worried that their job will be replaced by technology within two years, according to PwC. And the World Economic Forum says that by 2027, the occupation with the largest net job growth will be "AI and Machine Learning Specialist."

CEOs are already warning their workers. "Artificial intelligence is going to replace literally half of all white-collar workers in the U.S.," says Ford CEO Jim Farley. Marianne Lake, CEO of JPMorgan Chase's consumer and community business, said in 2025 that her staff will be reduced by 10% in coming years as the company turns to AI. Anthropic CEO Dario Amodei has said that half of all entry-level jobs could disappear by 2030, resulting in an unemployment rate as high as 20%. Micha Kaufman, CEO of Fiverr, sent an email to staff in 2025 saying, "This is a wake-up call. It does not matter if you are a programmer, designer, product manager, data scientist, lawyer, customer support rep, salesperson, or a finance person—AI is coming for you."

Shopify CEO Tobi Lütke told his team they aren't allowed to hire anyone without first proving that AI can't do the job, while ThredUp CEO James Reinhart told his staff, "I think AI is going to destroy way more jobs than the average person thinks." IBM CEO Arvind Krishna says his company has already used AI to replace hundreds of people in its human resources department, and Amazon CEO Andy Jassy wrote in an email to his 1.6 million employees that AI could displace them. "We will need fewer people doing some of the jobs that are being done today, and more people doing other types of jobs," he wrote. Make sure the degree you choose to get is among the latter that Jassy referred to, not the former.

After all, many skilled occupations have already vanished, including these:

- Alewife – a woman who brewed and sold ale
- Alnager – an official responsible for inspecting the shape and quality of woolen cloth
- Armorer – a skilled metalworker who makes suits of armor, much like a tailor
- Brush-maker – a person who manufactured brushes, brooms and mops
- Buckle-maker – a person who made metal buckles for shoes, harnesses, saddles and more
- Coach-maker – a person who constructed horse-drawn carriages
- Computer – a human who created mathematical tables used in astronomy, weather forecasting and other fields

- Cooper – a craftsman who produced wooden casks, barrels and other containers
- Drummer – a person who conveyed signals to troops on the battlefield
- Elocutionist – a speaker and entertainer who read passages from books with animated gestures
- Keypunch operator – a person who entered data or programs onto cards by punching holes in them so the cards could be read by computers (machines, not humans)
- Scribe – a professional who copied manuscripts prior to the invention of Gutenberg's printer
- Switchboard operator – a person who connected someone to another by making telephone calls with the person they were trying to reach
- Telegraph operator – a person who sent and received messages via a wire laid over long distances
- Town crier – an officer or public authority who made public announcements by shouting in the streets
- Wheelwright – an artisan who built or repaired wooden wheels for horse-drawn carriages

All these occupations, and hundreds more, required skilled workers who often served as apprentices for a decade or more to learn their craft. Yet, their jobs were eliminated when superior technology was invented. This is now happening to accountants and thousands of other high-paying jobs.

Table 10.4 lists the jobs that people go to college to learn about but that Oxford University says have a 90% or higher probability of being eliminated due to technology over the next decade.

Table 10.4 It's Highly Likely That These Jobs Won't Exist in 10 Years

- Accountants and Auditors
- Adhesive Bonding Machine Operators and Tenders
- Agricultural and Food Science Technicians
- Agricultural Inspectors
- Animal Breeders
- Appraisers and Assessors of Real Estate
- Automotive Body and Related Repairers
- Bicycle Repairers
- Bill and Account Collectors
- Billing and Posting Clerks
- Bookkeeping, Accounting and Auditing Clerks
- Bridge and Lock Tenders
- Brokerage Clerks
- Budget Analysts
- Butchers and Meat Cutters
- Cabinetmakers and Bench Carpenters
- Camera and Photographic Equipment Repairers
- Cargo and Freight Agents
- Cashiers
- Cement Masons and Concrete Finishers
- Claims Adjusters, Examiners and Investigators
- Coating, Painting and Spraying Machine Setters, Operators and Tenders
- Coin, Vending, and Amusement Machine Servicers and Repairers
- Combined Food Preparation and Serving Workers, Including Fast Food
- Compensation and Benefits Managers
- Conveyor Operators and Tenders
- Cooks, Restaurant
- Cooks, Short Order
- Cooling and Freezing Equipment Operators and Tenders
- Counter and Rental Clerks
- Counter Attendants, Cafeteria, Food Concession and Coffee Shop
- Couriers and Messengers
- Crane and Tower Operators
- Credit Analysts
- Credit Authorizers, Checkers and Clerks
- Crushing, Grinding and Polishing Machine Setters, Operators and Tenders
- Data Entry Keyers
- Dental Laboratory Technicians
- Dining Room and Cafeteria Attendants and Bartender Helpers
- Dispatchers, Except Police, Fire and Ambulance
- Door-to-Door Sales Workers, News and Street Vendors, and Related Workers
- Dredge Operators

(Continued)

Table 10.4 (Continued)

- Drilling and Boring Machine Tool Setters, Operators and Tenders – Metal and Plastic
- Driver/Sales Workers
- Electrical and Electronic Equipment Assemblers
- Electrical and Electronics Installers and Repairers, Transportation Equipment
- Electromechanical Equipment Assemblers
- Etchers and Engravers
- Excavating and Loading Machine and Dragline Operators
- Extruding and Drawing Machine Setters, Operators and Tenders – Metal and Plastic
- Extruding, Forming, Pressing and Compacting Machine Setters, Operators and Tenders
- Fabric Menders, Except Garment
- Farm Labor Contractors
- Fence Erectors
- Fiberglass Laminators and Fabricators
- File Clerks
- First-Line Supervisors of Housekeeping and Janitorial Workers
- Food and Tobacco Roasting, Baking and Drying Machine Operators and Tenders
- Forging Machine Setters, Operators and Tenders – Metal and Plastic
- Gaming and Sports Book Writers and Runners
- Gaming Dealers
- Gaming Surveillance Officers and Gaming Investigators
- Gas Compressor and Gas Pumping Station Operators
- Geological and Petroleum Technicians
- Grinding and Polishing Workers, Hand
- Grinding, Lapping, Polishing and Buffing Machine Tool Setters, Operators and Tenders – Metal and Plastic
- Heat Treating Equipment Setters, Operators and Tenders – Metal and Plastic
- Helpers–Carpenters
- Helpers–Painters, Paperhangers, Plasterers and Stucco Masons
- Hosts and Hostesses, Restaurant, Lounge and Coffee Shop
- Hotel, Motel and Resort Desk Clerks
- Human Resources Assistants, Except Payroll and Timekeeping
- Industrial Truck and Tractor Operators
- Inspectors, Testers, Sorters, Samplers and Weighers
- Insurance Appraisers, Auto Damage
- Insurance Claims and Policy Processing Clerks
- Insurance Sales Agents
- Insurance Underwriters
- Interviewers, Except Eligibility and Loan
- Jewelers and Precious Stone and Metal Workers

- Landscaping and Groundskeeping Workers
- Legal Secretaries
- Library Assistants, Clerical
- Library Technicians
- Loan Interviewers and Clerks
- Loan Officers
- Locomotive Engineers
- Locomotive Firers
- Log Graders and Scalers
- Machine Feeders and Offbearers
- Mail Clerks and Mail Machine Operators, Except Postal Service
- Manicurists and Pedicurists
- Mathematical Technicians
- Meat, Poultry and Fish Cutters and Trimmers
- Mechanical Door Repairers
- Medical and Clinical Laboratory Technologists
- Medical Records and Health Information Technicians
- Milling and Planing Machine Setters, Operators and Tenders – Metal and Plastic
- Model Makers – Metal and Plastic
- Model Makers – Wood
- Models
- Molders, Shapers, and Casters, Except Metal and Plastic
- Molding, Coremaking and Casting Machine Setters, Operators and Tenders – Metal and Plastic
- Motion Picture Projectionists
- Multiple Machine Tool Setters, Operators and Tenders – Metal and Plastic
- Musical Instrument Repairers and Tuners
- New Accounts Clerks
- Nuclear Power Reactor Operators
- Office Clerks, General
- Office Machine Operators, Except Computer
- Operating Engineers and Other Construction Equipment Operators
- Ophthalmic Laboratory Technicians
- Order Clerks
- Outdoor Power Equipment and Other Small Engine Mechanics
- Packaging and Filling Machine Operators and Tenders
- Painting, Coating and Decorating Workers
- Paralegals and Legal Assistants
- Parts Salespersons
- Patternmakers – Metal and Plastic
- Patternmakers – Wood
- Payroll and Timekeeping Clerks
- Pesticide Handlers, Sprayers and Applicators, Vegetation
- Pharmacy Technicians
- Photographic Process Workers and Processing Machine Operators
- Plating and Coating Machine Setters, Operators and Tenders – Metal and Plastic
- Postal Service Clerks
- Prepress Technicians and Workers
- Print Binding and Finishing Workers
- Procurement Clerks
- Production Workers, All Other
- Pump Operators, Except Wellhead Pumpers

(Continued)

Table 10.4 (*Continued*)

- Radio Operators
- Radio, Cellular and Tower Equipment Installers and Repairers
- Rail Yard Engineers, Dinkey Operators and Hostlers
- Real Estate Brokers
- Receptionists and Information Clerks
- Refuse and Recyclable Material Collectors
- Reinforcing Iron and Rebar Workers
- Retail Salespersons
- Rock Splitters, Quarry
- Roofers
- Secretaries and Administrative Assistants, Except Legal, Medical and Executive
- Service Unit Operators, Oil, Gas and Mining
- Sewers, Hand
- Shipping, Receiving, and Traffic Clerks
- Shoe Machine Operators and Tenders
- Signal and Track Switch Repairers
- Surveying and Mapping Technicians
- Switchboard Operators, Including Answering Service
- Tax Examiners and Collectors, and Revenue Agents
- Tax Preparers
- Team Assemblers
- Telemarketers
- Telephone Operators
- Tellers
- Textile Bleaching and Dyeing Machine Operators and Tenders
- Textile Cutting Machine Setters, Operators and Tenders
- Textile Winding, Twisting, and Drawing Out Machine Setters, Operators and Tenders
- Timing Device Assemblers and Adjusters
- Tire Builders
- Title Examiners, Abstractors and Searchers
- Tour Guides and Escorts
- Traffic Technicians
- Transportation Inspectors
- Umpires, Referees and Other Sports Officials
- Ushers, Lobby Attendants and Ticket Takers
- Waiters and Waitresses
- Watch Repairers
- Weighers, Measurers, Checkers and Samplers, Recordkeeping
- Welders, Cutters, Solderers and Brazers
- Woodworking Machine Setters, Operators and Tenders

You can see why Goldman Sachs says 300 million full-time jobs could be automated by AI and why PWC found in 2024 that 25% of the 5,000 biggest companies in 105 countries were starting to lay off at least 5% of their workforce.

But at the same time, 70% of the CEOs at those companies said, by 2027, AI will force them to hire an entirely new category of workers – demonstrating that AI will create jobs, not merely eliminate them. In addition to that, Oxford University says lots of today's occupations will persist, including those listed in Table 10.5 – all of which will continue to require a college degree.

Table 10.5   These Jobs Are Probably Here to Stay – and Will Require That You Have a College Degree

- Advertising and Promotions Managers
- Aerospace Engineers
- Agents
- Aircraft Cargo Handling Supervisors
- Animal Scientists
- Animal Trainers
- Anthropologists
- Applications Developers
- Arbitrators, Mediators and Conciliators
- Archeologists
- Architects, Except Landscape and Naval
- Architectural and Engineering Managers
- Art Directors
- Astronomers
- Athletes And Sports Competitors
- Athletic Trainers, Coaches and Scouts
- Audiologists
- Biochemists and Biophysicists
- Biological Scientists
- Biomedical Engineers
- Business Intelligence Analysts
- Business Managers
- Chefs and Head Cooks
- Chemical Engineers
- Chemists
- Chief Executives
- Childcare Workers
- Chiropractors

(Continued)

Table 10.5   (Continued)

- Choreographers
- Civil Engineers
- Clergy
- Coaches and Scouts
- Commercial and Industrial Designers
- Community Service Managers
- Compliance Officers
- Computer and Information Scientists and Analysts
- Computer Scientists
- Concierges
- Conservation Scientists
- Construction Managers
- Construction Workers
- Craft Artists
- Credit Counselors
- Curators
- Database Administrators
- Dentists
- Dietitians
- Editors
- Education Administrators
- Electrical Power-Line Installers and Repairers
- Electronics Engineers
- Emergency Management Directors
- Emergency Medical Technicians and Paramedics
- Engineers
- Ethicists
- Event Planners
- Fabric and Apparel Patternmakers
- Farm and Home Management Advisors
- Farmers, Ranchers and Other Agricultural Managers
- Fashion Designers
- Financial Managers
- Fine Artists, including Painters, Sculptors and Illustrators
- Firefighters
- First-Line Supervisors
- Fish and Game Wardens
- Fitness Trainers and Aerobics Instructors
- Flight Attendants
- Floral Designers
- Food Scientists and Technologists
- Food Service Managers
- Forensic Science Technicians
- Forest Fire Inspectors and Prevention Specialists
- Foresters
- Fundraising Managers
- Gamification Designers
- Gaming Managers
- Geographers
- Graphic Designers
- Guidance Counselors
- Hairdressers
- Health and Safety Engineers
- Health Diagnosing and Treating Practitioners
- Healthcare Practitioners and Technical Workers
- Human Resources Managers and Specialists
- Hydrologists

- Industrial Engineers and Technicians
- Industrial Production Managers
- Instructional Coordinators
- Interior Designers
- Landscape Architects
- Lawyers
- Lodging Managers
- Logisticians
- Makeup Artists
- Managers and Analysts
- Marine Engineers
- Market Research Analysts
- Marketing Managers
- Marriage and Family Therapists
- Materials Engineers and Scientists
- Mathematicians
- Mechanical Engineers
- Medical and Health Services Managers
- Medical Scientists
- Mental Health Counselors
- Microbiologists
- Multimedia Artists and Animators
- Musical Directors, Composers and Singers
- Natural Sciences Managers
- Naval Architects
- Network and Computer Systems Administrators
- Nuclear Engineers
- Nurses
- Nutritionists
- Occupational Therapists and Assistants
- Operations Research Analysts
- Orthodontists, Orthotists and Prosthetists
- Pharmacists
- Photographers
- Physical Therapists and Assistants
- Physicians
- Physicists
- Podiatrists
- Police and Sheriff's Officers
- Political Scientists
- Private Detectives
- Producers and Directors
- Project Managers
- Prosthodontists
- Psychiatric Technicians
- Psychologists
- Public Relations Managers and Specialists
- Purchasing Managers
- Radio and Television News Analysts and Announcers
- Recreation Workers
- Rehabilitation Counselors
- Religious Activities Directors
- Religious Educators
- Residential Advisors
- Robotics Specialists
- Sales Reps, Engineers and Managers
- Scientists
- Securities, Commodities and Financial Services Sales Agents
- Set and Exhibit Designers
- Ship Engineers
- Social and Community Service Managers

(Continued)

Table 10.5 (*Continued*)

- Social Scientists and Related Workers
- Sociologists
- Software Developers
- Soil and Plant Scientists
- Speech-Language Pathologists
- Substance Abuse and Behavioral Disorder Counselors
- Substance Abuse Counselors
- Surgeons
- Teachers
- Therapists and Therapy Technicians
- Training and Development Managers and Specialists
- Travel Agents and Guides
- Veterinarians
- Veterinarians and Veterinary Technologists and Technicians
- Web Developers
- Writers and Authors
- Zoologists

So, make sure you choose a field that will survive and thrive in tomorrow's technological society. Essentially, the skills that will be valued most are **thinking, creating, communicating** and **managing** – so take courses that teach you these skills. And revisit the sidebar earlier in this chapter on page 123.

9. They don't consider apprenticeships instead of college

Apprenticeships, a centuries-old approach to learning skills, have been eclipsed by the more formal education provided by institutions of higher education. But the downsides of college – the time, cost and concern that students aren't taught the skills needed to succeed in today's workforce (as we learned in Chapter 3) – have led to a renewed interest in apprenticeships.

Indeed, there are now 64% more of these programs than 10 years ago, says the Department of Labor, because employers have discovered their value. SHRM, formerly the Society for Human Resource Management, reports that 94% of executives, 93% of supervisors and 91% of HR professionals say they see little difference between job candidates who have a college degree and people who have a certificate earned via an apprenticeship. Google, Delta, IBM and many other employers have stopped requiring a bachelor's degree for certain jobs. Instead, they say, what matters is skill and experience – something apprenticeships deliver. They do that by providing both on-the-job training and classroom instruction, in programs that last from 12 months to 6 years.

It's easy to see why this idea makes sense. Instead of paying for college, employers (desperate for skilled labor) pay you a salary while you get trained. You interact with professionals while you're learning, helping you build connections that can help in your future career, and you often receive a certification upon completion which validates your skills (like a degree is supposed to do). Best yet, the employer that's paid your salary and trained you is highly likely to offer you a job when your training is complete. What's not to love?

We're not just talking about trades like plumbing and carpentry. Consider LVMH, owner of 75 of the most prestigious luxury brands in the world, such as Louis Vuitton, Christian Dior, Givenchy, Fendi, Dom Pérignon, TAG Heuer, Bulgari, Tiffany and more. In 2024, LVMH hired 60,000 people, including 3,500 artisanal workers.

Most of these people must be trained because it takes 15 hours to make a single Hermes handbag – and no college teaches those skills. Hermes offers high salaries and annual bonuses equal to 150% of pay. This is just one example of the value of education that you can get outside of the standard college path.

If you're interested in pursuing an apprenticeship, start like you would with the college path: Decide which fields and jobs interest you. You'll find that apprenticeships are available in almost every field – construction, health care (nursing, dental assisting and medical coding), technology (IT support, cybersecurity and software development), business and finance, creative fields (graphic design, media production and fashion) and more.

With a career in mind, visit Apprenticeship.gov, hosted by the Department of Labor, for a list of opportunities. If there's a specific company you want to work for, visit its website to see if apprenticeships are offered.

You can also search the web to discover such programs as the "Heavy Metal Summer Experience," a nonprofit summer camp that operates in 51 locations nationwide. It's free, hosted by local contractors.

Also, every industry has a "trade association," a group organized to help all the businesses in that industry prosper. For example, Associated Builders and Contractors lets you know of apprenticeships available at construction companies nationwide. Community colleges and vocational schools often partner with employers to offer apprenticeships, too, so contact those where you live. And of course, check out job and career sites like Indeed, LinkedIn and Glassdoor.

Too many high school students are unfamiliar with apprenticeships and therefore don't consider them. Be sure you do.

10. They fail to consider the lifestyle that their career choice will impose

Let's assume you can obtain the job of your dreams. Are you sure you'll like it? I'm not asking about the job; I'm asking about the lifestyle that the job gives you.

Ever since you were a child, adults have asked you, "What do you want to be when you grow up?" They should have asked, "When you grow up, what kind of lifestyle do you want to live?" because this question is far more important. So, let's talk about it.

Make no mistake, the job you get upon graduation will determine:

- The time you wake up
- The clothes you wear
- The place you go each workday
- The people you spend 8–10 hours with each workday
- When you eat, where you eat, who you eat with and how much you spend to eat

By extension, the job will also be a major factor in determining:

- Your friends
- Who you marry
- When and how many children you have
- Where you live, the cost and type of housing and whether you rent or buy your home
- How often you see your family

And, your job will determine every other aspect of your "material" (meaning *purchased*) life, because your salary will determine what you can afford to buy – a Swatch versus a Rolex, a used Chevy versus a new BMW, a cramped basement apartment versus a spacious house with a yard.

In addition, your job will determine the city (or country) you'll live in, whether you work 9 a.m. to 5 p.m. Monday through Friday or very different hours. Some jobs can be performed remotely; some employers are happy to let you live and work anywhere, provided you perform well. But even though a given job can be done anywhere, many employers demand that you be at the workplace every workday. And being at the workplace is required for many jobs; schoolteachers and surgical nurses can't do their jobs from home.

So, ask yourself these five questions:

1. **How do you feel about working remotely?** Some employers refuse it, others permit it and still others require it. Do the opportunities and restrictions related to remote work match your career aspirations?

2. **What hours do you want to work?** Some jobs require that you work nights (10 p.m. to 6 a.m.) or weekends. Others rely on shift work, meaning your work hours cycle across the 24-hour clock every three weeks.

    Some sectors, such as retail, hospitality, health care and law enforcement, demand that you work weekends and holidays. Are you OK with working instead of being with family and friends on Thanksgiving, Christmas and New Year's? You might like the idea of being an emergency room nurse, but are you prepared to work 16-hour double shifts during the holidays? If you aspire to be the meteorologist for a local TV news station, you may find yourself waking at 2 a.m. so you can be on-air by 4 a.m. You'll be off-air by 10 a.m. and off duty by noon. You'll have dinner at 2 p.m. and go to bed at 6 p.m. The only people you'll socialize with are others with similar schedules. But you'll be totally out of sync with your spouse and children. Are you OK with this?

3. **How much travel is required?** Some jobs demand much, others none. If your job requires travel, understand the details. Will you have a big expense account or a strict budget? Will you be sent to dangerous parts of the world? How often will you be on the road, and what stress might this put on your relationships (or even your ability to form them)?

4. **How long will it take for you to get the job you really want?** It often takes years, even decades, to get the job of your dreams; are you willing to work in that field for as long as it takes, even with no guarantee of ever getting the position you truly want?

5. **What compensation can you realistically expect from this career?** You'll inevitably find out, so it's best that you do *before* you select a major or college. I once chatted with a gentleman who was looking for a new job. He had graduated four years earlier and quickly got a good job in his chosen field. His starting salary was $40,000. He could thus afford only a small apartment, didn't own a car, struggled to pay his monthly bills and never had money to save. But the job gave him the opportunity to gain experience, which would lead to promotions

and, he figured, a much higher income. But a few months earlier, he attended an industry conference where he met folks in the same field who are 20 years older. He learned that these executives – who held the jobs he aspired to attain – were each earning about $60,000.

That news hit him hard. *I have to work for 20 years and merely hope to get a $60,000 salary?*

He had no idea that his chosen career offered such low compensation potential. Although he enjoyed his field, he realized it would never provide the lifestyle he wanted. This forced him to admit that this career would not be fulfilling, and he thus regretted his decision to major in a field that doesn't offer the income potential he wanted. By the time I met him, he was looking for a new job and had no idea what field he might end up in.

One day, you'll discover the potential compensation your field offers. That day will either be today or after you graduate from college. I recommend you choose today.

11. They don't realize that the school they've selected might close

In 2025, there were 1.3 million fewer students attending college than in 2021. That's $65 billion in lost tuition revenue for colleges and universities.

The impact? Hundreds of them are expected to close over the next decade. In fact, dozens closed in 2024 and 2025, including Presentation College in South Dakota, Cazenovia College in New York, Holy Names University in California, Living Arts College in North Carolina and Milwaukee's Cardinal Stritch University, founded in 1937.

Never heard of them? Well, perhaps you're familiar with the University of Nebraska, Rutgers, Penn State and the University of Minnesota. These Big Ten schools have all announced they're in financial trouble: The University of Nebraska has a $13 million budget deficit; Rutgers University's is $125 million; Penn State is short by $140 million; and the University of Minnesota says it needs $300 million. If these Big Ten schools are in such dire financial condition, how must the country's thousands of smaller schools be faring?

This situation has developed because institutions of higher education have borrowed billions of dollars since 2000, increasing their annual spending by 38%, according to the *Wall Street Journal*, and they're now struggling to repay their debts. The University of Kentucky spent $3.7 billion on a student center, a 900-space parking garage, a video game competition theater and dorms where every room has full-size Tempur-Pedic mattresses, granite countertops and washer/dryers. It costs $36,640 to attend UK even though its students hail from one of the poorest states in the country.

UK is not alone. The University of Oklahoma spent $14 million to buy and renovate a 32,000-square-foot monastery in Italy for its study-abroad program. The monastery now features a landscaped garden, faculty apartments and classrooms with painted frescoes; every OU student – not just those spending a semester in Italy – are paying higher tuition to cover this expense.

State colleges and universities aren't in financial trouble merely because of their spending; state legislatures have been cutting education budgets for two decades. But this hasn't caused schools to reduce their spending; instead, for every dollar they've lost in state funding, they've raised tuition and fees by $2.40, according to the WSJ. And much of that money has been spent on items unrelated to education, such as sports programs, dorms and stadiums. As I described in my book, *The Truth About Your Future*, Boston University students live in a 26-story glass and steel tower featuring walk-in closets and floor-length mirrors. The Indiana University of Pennsylvania spent $270 million on residence halls complete with private bedrooms and bathrooms, microwave ovens, refrigerators and carpeting. Gettysburg College's $27 million, 55,000 square-foot recreation center has a rock-climbing wall. Drexel University's $45 million, 84,000 square-foot recreation center has a walking and jogging track. The University of Memphis has a $50 million, 169,000 square-foot campus center with a movie theater and food court. The University of Alabama, Boston University, and Texas Tech each has a lazy river. And High Point University offers students a first-run movie theater, steakhouse, outdoor hot tubs, free food, a roaming ice cream truck and a concierge desk. It even employs a Director of Wow. No wonder the book *College (Un)bound* says college students spend 3.3 times as many hours in social and recreational activities as they do in classes, labs and studying. With all that fun being offered, which would you rather do?

All these non-academic programs need staff to operate them. That explains why, according to the WSJ, the number of administrators has skyrocketed over the past two decades while faculty ranks haven't changed. The University of Florida reportedly has more than 50 directors, associate directors and assistant directors of communication – twice as many as it did in 2017. The school also has more than 160 deans.

The students at these and other schools are feeling the pain. Penn State's spending is up 36% since 2002 and its tuition is up 72%. West Virginia University fired 169 faculty members (7% of the total) to help reduce its $45 million budget shortfall. It also shut down 32 of its 338 majors, leaving hundreds of students without a clear path to a degree.

Imagine you're attending a college that, without warning, eliminates your major and fires your professors. Or, worse, it announces that the entire college is closing at the end of the academic year. You've spent tens of thousands of dollars over three or four years so far at this college. The elimination of your major, or the school's outright closure, means you can't return in the fall to continue or complete your education.

This has happened to more than one million college students. If you find yourself hapless among them, you must apply to other colleges and hope they'll accept you. Even if they do, you'll have to retake most of your classes, because the Government Accountability Office says colleges accept just 43% of the credits that students earned elsewhere. That translates into an extra year or two of college for you, tens of thousands of dollars in additional costs and potentially hundreds of thousands of dollars in lost retirement savings because of your delay in entering the workforce.

This is why tens of thousands of students who experience this fiasco choose not to transfer. Instead, they simply . . . drop out. But they must still repay all the student loans they've obtained.

From 2000 to 2010, colleges were closing at the rate of about one a month. They're now closing at the rate of one a week, and 10% are in "immediate financial peril" according to E&Y. And students are always the last to know. (The University of the Arts in Philadelphia, a 150-year-old institution, announced in May 2024 that it was closing – and did so just a week later. Birmingham Southern College closed on May 31, 2024, with no notice; its varsity baseball team was playing in the Intercollegiate World Series Championship in Ohio and there was no college for the students to return to.) In fact, of all the colleges that have closed since 2020, 70% did so with no warning, according to the Hechinger Report, affecting 1.25 million students.

Even the most prominent institutions are facing financial upheaval, now that President Trump is holding them accountable for their anti-semitic and discriminatory policies and behaviors. Harvard President Alan Garber warned of "disruptive changes, painful layoffs and ongoing uncertainty" should the school lose the $1 billion that the president has threatened to withhold. Stanford University President Jon Levin said the resulting $140 million budget cut would include faculty layoffs. Columbia University Acting President Claire Shipman said the cancellation of $400 million in federal funding would "immediately impact students." And UCLA President James Milliken said any federal funds suspension "would completely devastate our country's greatest public university system as well as inflict great harm on our students."

So, before you apply to any college or university, you need to examine its financial status. Here are seven strategies that can help you ascertain a given institution's health.

1. Have there been any accreditation sanctions?

Do not apply to any college that isn't accredited or whose accreditations have been revoked, suspended or threatened. Ask the school for a list of its accreditations; contact those bodies to confirm the school's status and add your contact information to their distribution lists so you're updated if there's news.

2. Check with the institution's bond issuers: If the school has missed any payments, runaway

Quick lesson here. If you want to borrow five bucks, you ask a friend or family member. If you want to borrow five grand, you ask a bank for a loan. But if you want to borrow fifty million, you turn to the bond market. That's where governments, corporations and institutions (like colleges and universities) borrow massive sums of money.

It's vitally important to everyone that the school honor its obligations. If it doesn't make each interest payment on time or if it fails to return the principal at maturity, investors won't be so willing to buy more of its bonds in the future. That could cause the school to close.

> Here's how that works. A school hires a Wall Street firm to issue bonds on its behalf. Each bond costs $10,000 (called *principal*), so if the school needs $50 million, it'll sell 5,000 bonds. The Wall Street firm sells the bonds to its clients (*investors*). The school gets the proceeds minus the brokerage firm's commission (*underwriting fee*) and pays income (*interest*) to the investors semi-annually for a set period, usually 30 years (*maturity date*). Upon maturity, the school returns the principal to the investors. The school presumably spent that $50 million, so where does it get the cash to return all that money to investors upon maturity? By issuing new bonds!

This is why analysts in the financial services industry monitor the bond market closely. You can call pretty much any financial advisor to find out if a given school has failed to pay interest or principal in the past five years. If you discover this has happened, it means the school is in severe financial difficulty. Do not apply or enroll there.

3. Examine the school's KPIs

If you want to know whether a college is financially strong, examine information that the business community calls *Key Performance Indicators*. Three resources are:

- **The Common Data Set.** Published annually by many colleges and universities, it provides statistics on enrollment, admissions, financial aid, merit awards and more. You'll find the CDSs on each school's website or simply search the web. They all use a standard format, making it easy to compare data.

- **The U.S. Department of Education's Integrated Postsecondary Education Data System.** This database provides financial information on thousands of colleges.
- **IRS Form 990.** All nonprofit colleges submit this form to the Internal Revenue Service annually; the data often provides more information than the schools' published financial statements. Instead of searching the IRS website for each school you're interested in, use https://projects.propublica.org/nonprofits/. (Note: although state schools are technically nonprofits, they're government entities so they aren't required to file 990s. Still, many of them do.)

With the data in hand, here's what you want to do:

1. Look at the school's financial condition.

Gather information about the institution's:

- Annual budget and total income from all non-tuition sources (such as student fees, state funding, distributions from its endowment and ticket sales from athletic programs)
- Average tuition actually paid by full-time students (few pay the listed amount; most pay sharply discounted rates, thanks to scholarships and grants)
- Number of full-time students

Then, do two quick arithmetic puzzles:

> Budget
> − Income from Non-Tuition Sources
> = Tuition Income Needed

> Average Tuition
> × Number of Students
> = Total Tuition Income

Then, simply compare the two sums. The bigger the gap, the bigger the school's financial problems.

Has the school's net income been declining for years? That's a bad sign; while colleges aren't trying to earn a big profit, they do need some gains to remain financially solvent. Posting losses year after year inevitably results in closure.

2. Examine student enrollment data.

Forty percent of the nation's colleges are rural liberal arts institutions with fewer than 1,000 students, according to the National Center for Education Statistics. E&Y says most of these schools won't exist by 2035, because their small student population generates insufficient tuition revenue.

3. Compare student enrollment to 20 years ago.

It's bad for a college to have a small number of students. It's worse if the college's student body has been declining. Newbury College in Boston had 5,300 students in 2000, but just 600 by the time it closed in 2024. Just as restaurants can't stay in business without enough diners, colleges can't remain open without enough students. So, check to see if enrollments have been declining.

4. Examine enrollment in your planned field of study.

Even if there hasn't been a decline in the overall student population, look closely at the roster in your major. If that enrollment is low, or high but falling, your school might terminate the program before you graduate, forcing you to transfer. Or it might fire your department's faculty to save money – and gutting the program could leave you with a degree from an institution that employers dislike. Don't be fooled by numbers that show an increase in enrollment in your major, either, because that could be the result of tuition discounts (see the next item).

5. Examine the extent of tuition discounts.

You might be thrilled to receive the offer of a full scholarship. But you must ask how common such offers are. It could be that the school is desperate for students to enroll – and it could be using money from its small endowment fund or newly obtained loans from recent bond offerings to dangle that tantalizing offer.

A full scholarship is good for you, but it's bad for the school, because your attendance represents no revenue for the institution. Too many free rides can translate into financial strife for the college or university. So, find out if the school has increased its spending on scholarships in the past decade. If it has, then either the school is fabulously wealthy (Johns Hopkins University's medical school is now free, thanks to a $1 billion gift from Bloomberg founder and former New York City mayor Michael Bloomberg) – or financially unstable. Find out which it is.

Schools that give big tuition discounts to lots of students figure it's better to get a little revenue from incoming freshmen than have them go elsewhere and get nothing. That sort of logic usually ends with a school closing.

4. Does the school have an endowment fund?

You've probably heard of Harvard's endowment fund. It's the largest in higher education, more than $53 billion at this writing. The combined endowments of the eight Ivy League schools (Harvard, Yale, Princeton, University of Pennsylvania, Columbia, Cornell, Dartmouth and Brown) exceed $200 billion.

Endowment funds operate independently from their schools. They receive donations (mostly from alumni) and invest the money so the fund will rise in value. Each year, they distribute a portion of the fund's assets to their schools, which add the proceeds to their budgets.

Although there's more than $1 trillion in university endowments nationwide, just 120 schools have 75% of the money. So, it's worth asking the schools you plan to apply to if they have an endowment fund. And if so:

- *What is the size of the endowment?* A small endowment suggests that alumni are not engaged with the institution. Perhaps that suggests they weren't thrilled with their experience.

- *How many alumni donated to it last year, and what was the average contribution?* A big endowment could be the result of one wealthy benefactor. See how extensively the alumni support the endowment.
- *What percentage of the endowment was distributed to the school in each of the past 10 years, and what percentage of the school's budget did that money represent?* Endowment funds usually distribute just 5% of their money to their schools each year, but they sometimes agree to make larger distributions. That's fine, provided it doesn't put the endowment at risk of running out of money. In the two years before it closed, for example, Birmingham-Southern College received $28 million from its $52 million endowment. This not only decimated the fund, it also provided ample evidence that the college was in big financial trouble.
- *What percentage of the endowment's funds are restricted?* Many alumni require that the money they donate be used for specific purposes, such as scholarships or funding a faculty position. Those donations can't be helpful to the school if it encounters financial difficulties.

5. How many presidents have served in the past 10 years?

The average college president serves for six years, according to the American Council of Education. So, if a college you're considering has had three or four presidents in the past decade, you must wonder why. Better yet, don't wonder. Just go to a different school.

And it's not just the president's office that might be problematic. Ask about all the top leadership positions, including:

- *Provost:* The second-highest position in higher education; leads academic deans and administrators.
- *Chief Academic Officer:* Ensures that academic programs meet accreditation as well as state and federal requirements.
- *Dean:* Each is responsible for a given department (or, for universities, school).
- *Department Head or Chair:* The second-highest position in a department or school.
- *Director of Admissions:* Leads the function of selecting which student applicants are invited to enroll.
- *Director of Academic Advising:* Collaborates with faculty to help students stay in school and complete their degrees.
- *Director of Career Services:* Leads the team that helps students and alumni find jobs and advance in their careers.
- *Director of Alumni Relations:* Develops and implements strategies to keep alumni engaged with the institution, often coordinating with the chief development officer,
- *Chief Development Officer:* Responsible for raising money from donors, often for the endowment. College presidents also devote a significant part of their time to fundraising.

Frequent turnover among college leadership suggests that there may be severe conflicts with the board, perhaps over money (or the lack of it) or strategy (such as whether to start or close an academic program). Such turmoil could translate into major disruption in your college experience.

A subtle but important indication of a leadership gap is over-reliance on consultants. You'll have to pore through disclosures, such as the minutes of trustee board meetings or vendor payments listed by nonprofit institutions in their Form 990 submissions.

If all this sounds like a lot of hassle, consider how much hassle it will be to find another school after yours shuts down.

6. Have a critical eye during your campus visit

The college tour is a rite of passage in the college selection process. During the visit, where college tour guides strive to wow you, conduct a more sober examination. Ask yourself:

- *Are the buildings in good condition or is paint peeling everywhere?* Visit buildings that aren't on the tour, especially those that house the classes you'll be taking – and check out the restrooms.
- *Is construction underway?* Colleges and universities should always be in a state of reinvention, because of new technologies and industries. Be wary if there aren't any academic structures being built or renovated.
- *What's the construction for?* It's a red flag if the only construction is for non-academic functions, like sports facilities and other extracurricular activities. These are signs that the school is more interested in recruiting students than educating them.
- *How's the landscaping?* If you see signs of deferred maintenance – grass that needs seeding or mowing, cracked

sidewalks, pooled water – you're probably visiting a school that's experiencing budget cuts. Find a maintenance worker or someone on the grounds crew and ask if there have been staff or budget cuts in the past few years.

7. Check the news and code your news feeds to receive updates

Do an online search of the school's name combined with such words as *finances*, *enrollment* and *layoffs*.[9] Years before an institution closes, it'll experience layoffs, drops in enrollment and budget cuts. All these signs of financial trouble will have made the news, which means your web search will find them.

Also, activate an alert on your news feeds so you'll be informed about any developments affecting the school's finances.

12. They think colleges and universities are benevolent institutions, devoted to their best interests

It should be clear to you by now that institutions of higher education are not focused on your best interests.

---

[9] And while you do, keep in mind Ernest Hemingway's line about bankruptcy occurring "gradually and then suddenly."

If they were, they wouldn't be offering so many majors that don't prepare you for a successful career. One in four undergraduate degrees and 43% of master's degrees actually leave students worse off financially than if they'd not pursued that education, according to the Foundation for Research on Equal Opportunity. The organization examined Department of Education and Census Bureau data on 53,000 degrees and certificate programs and found that the cost of the degrees did not produce enough additional lifetime earnings to justify the cost.

So, if institutions of higher education were focused primarily on your best interests, they wouldn't be offering degrees that fail to improve your financial life. (If tobacco companies cared primarily about your health, they wouldn't sell cigarettes. But they want to maximize their revenue, so they sell products that aren't good for you. Colleges and universities do the same thing.)

And if those colleges and universities were focused primarily on your best interests, they wouldn't be charging you as much money as they do, and they wouldn't have policies and practices that increase your costs when they could just as easily create policies and procedures that reduce them.

If institutions of higher education were truly focused on their students' best interests, 24% of freshmen wouldn't drop out. The schools would work harder to graduate more students than the meager half who manage to do so after six years. They would prepare their students to succeed in life, and they would deliver degrees at the lowest cost possible.

But this isn't what colleges and universities focus on. Instead, they focus predominantly on staying open – and that means generating as much revenue as possible. So, they admit as many students as they can, whether or not those students are mentally, emotionally or academically likely to succeed, and then they charge as much money in tuition and fees as they can wrangle out of those students.

Every college knows it is competing for enrollments, so each does everything it can to entice you. The result is that colleges offer amenities that are completely unrelated to education but that are certainly appealing. Those recreation centers, movie theaters, hot tubs and lazy rivers are nothing more than drugs designed to turn a naïve high school senior into a credit-seeking addict. None of those features improves a student's knowledge or skills or prepares them to enter the workforce. Many schools would rather build a new football stadium than add a Nobel laureate to their faculty.

Here are four examples that prove colleges care more about what's best for them than their students:

1. More than one in five college students (22%) attend state colleges and universities outside their home state – and all these schools charge those out-of-state students much higher rates of tuition than in-state students. Consider two students, both enrolling as freshmen at Ohio State University. One pays $27,982 while the other pays $54,760. Why the difference? One resides in Ohio; the other doesn't.

    Some would argue that this is only fair since the family of the in-state student pays taxes that subsidize the cost of college. Fine, I'll buy that. But why does the college deny enrollment to so many Ohio applicants? Only 71% of the university's student population are from Ohio. Are the other 29% so much smarter or better qualified – or is it simply that the school wants them because it can collect twice as much money from them?

It's not my intention to single out OSU; nationally, 22% of college students are paying out-of-state rates. That means there are California kids going to school in Ohio, while Ohio kids go to school in California. It's foolish for the students to waste such money, and worse, it's unethical for the schools to let them.

The real tragedy of this policy: For every out-of-state student who gets accepted, there's an in-state student who gets rejected. This forces millions of applicants to attend out-of-state schools, paying out-of-state rates, even though they'd prefer not to. If the higher education system was truly focused on all students' best interests, it would not allow, let alone orchestrate, this behavior.

2. We've seen that students who transfer to another school must usually re-take their classes, because colleges accept only 43% of the credits that these students have. The colleges are clearly saying that they don't value the education you received at the former school. Why, then, are those same colleges willing to hire professors who graduated from those other colleges? Obviously, the colleges don't truly object to the education that other schools provide. They simply want to collect more tuition revenue from its transfer students. Again, whose interests are being served?

3. Almost all undergraduate degrees require 120 credits. Have colleges legitimately determined that mastery of every career – from teaching to biology to film production – is completed via *exactly* 120 credits, no more and no less? Or perhaps colleges have simply learned that they can generate more revenue by requiring all students to pay for 120 credits even though mastery of many subjects can be obtained with far fewer credits.

4. Published tuition rates at each college are almost always the same for every major. As a result, education majors usually pay the same to attend as engineering students – even though it costs a lot more to educate engineers than it does schoolteachers. (Teachers merely need classrooms with whiteboards; engineers need laboratories filled with technology.) And engineers earn far more than teachers – meaning lower-paid schoolteachers are typically subsidizing higher-paid engineers! This is completely backwards from the students' perspective, but it serves higher ed's business model.

Business model indeed. That's really my point: to help you realize that colleges and universities are nothing more than businesses, just like any other company. They have a product to sell (a college degree), and they package it as best they can to get you (the consumer) to buy it. Thus, be aware that when you're selecting a college, you're merely engaging in a business transaction.

Treat it as such.

In any business transaction, you must never believe that sellers are focused on what's best for the buyers. They aren't. They are focused on what's best for themselves.

This is not a condemnation of business; it's just the way it is – and it's best that you understand this before you begin engaging in the college selection (degree purchasing) process.

 **Key Takeaways**

1. Avoid the mistakes of others by doing the following:
   (a) Consider the type of employer you'd like to work for, and then see if such employers offer jobs in the field you're considering.
   (b) Find out if the career you want to pursue requires a college degree. If it doesn't, decide if the degree would be helpful enough to your success that obtaining it is nevertheless worthwhile.
   (c) Don't merely get a required degree; make sure you also get the skills you'll need to succeed in your career.
   (d) Before applying to college, confirm that the field you're planning to pursue has so many jobs available that it's more likely than not that you'll get one of them.
   (e) Find out if the field you're interested in requires a postgraduate degree or professional certification. If it does, decide now – before you apply to undergrad schools – if the additional years and costs are worthwhile. If the postgrad degree's ROI isn't worth it, then neither is the undergrad degree.
   (f) Evaluate the likelihood that technology will eliminate the career you're planning to pursue.
   (g) Consider an apprenticeship instead of college.

(Continued)

(Continued)
- **(h)** Think about the lifestyle your career choice will impose on you and your future family.
- **(i)** Evaluate the risk that the school you're planning to attend might close.
- **(j)** Keep in mind that colleges and universities are not benevolent institutions focused on your best interests. When shopping for an automobile, you wouldn't confide in the used-car sales rep you just met or assume they are telling you the truth. Treat every first contact in your college-decision journey with the same skepticism.

2. Most importantly, remember that the skills that will be valued in the job market are and will continue to be:
   - **(a)** Thinking
   - **(b)** Creating
   - **(c)** Communicating
   - **(d)** Managing

Therefore, take classes that teach you these skills.

Epilogue: College Is Out – Lifelong Learning Is In

Although this book has ostensibly been about college, it's really about your life. And that's why your desire to pursue an education beyond high school is not only admirable but essential.

That means you can't let college be the end point of your educational pursuits. Go back to Table 6.2 in Chapter 6. There's a data point embedded in that chart that I didn't mention: Those earning $100,000+ spend thousands of dollars annually on education, while those with lower incomes spend far less. College graduates are not only more likely to understand the value of education (leading them to continue learning throughout their lives by attending seminars and conferences, and completing certification courses in their field), they are also more financially able to do so.

Thus, education is not a synonym for college. Rather, it refers to *lifelong learning*. You've been in school since you were a toddler. You're in school today. And you'll still be in school in your early twenties. So, do as high-income people do: Whether or not you pursue and obtain a college degree, keep pursuing an education. You don't necessarily need to seek a master's or doctorate degree; simply *keep learning*. That's what wealthy people do – and if you do what they do, you'll increase your ability to become one of them.

And so, I've saved perhaps my most important message for you until the end: Regardless of the path you choose, the degree, certification or skills you obtain in your twenties will not be sufficient to ensure your success for the rest of your life.

This is an important point, so pause a moment to digest it. You see, back in the 1980s, you could get a degree in a given field and then spend an entire career in that occupation. But that's no longer the case. Today, due to the explosion in information being made possible by technological innovation, much of what you'll learn in your twenties will be out-of-date by your thirties.

Indeed, in 2016, then-CEO of AT&T Randall Stephenson said, "There is a need to retool yourself, and you should not expect to stop," adding that people who do not spend 5–10 hours a week in online learning "will obsolete themselves." And in 2017, Robert M. Lightfoot Jr., then head of NASA, said, "By the time you are a junior in college, what you learned as a freshman is already obsolete." Imagine how CEOs feel today about your need to have a current level of knowledge!

So, it's no longer enough to say you got a college degree from umpty-dump university a year (or decade) ago. Instead, you must make sure your knowledge and skills remain current – and that means you must continue your education. This is why you must replace the notion of a college degree with the concept of lifelong learning.

By developing this mindset, you'll realize that a college degree is merely a waypoint in your educational journey. And that realization will help you control both the costs and the outcome of that degree, so your life is better positioned upon its attainment than it was before you began. And this, my young friend, is the truth about college.

 **Key Takeaway**

1. Don't let college be the end point of your educational pursuits. Develop and maintain an engagement in lifelong learning.

20 Conversation Starters to Help Adults and Teenagers Talk About College

Now that you've finished the book, it's time to engage in conversation. Have the adult ask and the teenager respond to the following questions. If you're the adult, it's important that you express a non-judgmental tone and make it clear to the teen that there are no wrong answers. If you're the teen, you have my permission to demand that the adult behave accordingly. You both want an open, honest dialogue – with no adult insisting on a pre-ordained outcome.

There's no need to delve into all 20 of these questions, nor are you required to ask them in the order shown. And for sure, don't attempt to cover them all in a single conversation. Take as much time as you all need, focusing on the topics of greatest relevance and interest to the teenager.

A good idea, then, is for the teen to select the question(s) they want to discuss first. If there's more than one child in the household, you may find it best to include everyone in the dialogue; younger children and observers can benefit from listening to (and being part of) the conversation.

1. **What are your aspirations? Talk about the life you envision living once you're on your own. (Refer to Chapter 6.)**
   (a) **What did you think about Ric's description of the cost of living and the impact of taxes?**
      (i) **Did this content have any impact on how you've been thinking about the future?**
         It's quite possible, even likely, that teenagers haven't given this any thought – or any realistic thought anyway. Teens, you ought to ponder this for a while – perhaps over several days or weeks – before you start talking about it. Adults, check in with the teen periodically to help them stay focused on this question.
      (ii) **Did you know that so many people are dependent on government support? What do you think about that?**
         This is an opportunity to help the teen broaden their understanding of the world we live in. Different readers will respond differently in this conversation, depending on the degree to which they or their

families are receiving such support. It's a great opportunity to consider opposite points of view – the type of critical thinking that one is supposed to learn in college (but often doesn't).

  (b) Do you suppose that the career you're thinking of will support the kind of lifestyle you want to have? (Refer to Chapter 10.)
- (i) How do you feel about working remotely?
- (ii) What hours do you want to work?
- (iii) How much travel are you hoping or willing to do?
- (iv) How long will it take for you to get the job you really want?
- (v) What compensation can you realistically expect from this career?

2. Have any adults given you the impression that you're expected to follow a particular path, such as the following? (Refer to the preface.)
   - (a) Going or not going to college
   - (b) Pursuing or avoiding a particular career
   - (c) Attending or avoiding a particular college or university
   - (d) Attending or avoiding community college
   - (e) Whether you should live at home or at school while you go to college
   - (f) Whether you should or shouldn't work while you attend college
   - (g) Any other restrictions or parameters – such as cost or distance – regarding which school to attend

The teen's answers will help adults realize whether any manipulation has been going on. You adults might feel the teenager is making accusations; resist the urge to feel defensive. We're talking here about perceptions – and it's important that adults consider the teen's comments honestly and without being offended or reacting with recrimination.

3. **Is it important to you that you attend an out-of-state or private school? If so, why? (Refer to Chapter 10.)**
4. **What benefits of going to college matter the most to you? (Refer to Chapter 1.)**

    Some students highlight the pursuit of a certain career or the desire to combat a given social or global problem. But some students focus on partying – or simply the joy of not having to get a full-time job for the next six years. This is a great opportunity for adults to explore the teen's answers to this question and help them consider the impact that their viewpoint will have on their future.
5. **Ric talked a lot about how many students became miserable because they went to college. What was your reaction to that information? (Refer to Chapters 2 and 3.)**
6. **Is there any particular major or career path that you have in mind? How strongly do you think you're committed to it? (Refer to Chapters 4 and 5.)**
    (a) What interests you? What do you enjoy doing?
    (b) What *haven't* you considered?
    (c) Ric suggested that you determine if there are jobs available for what you want to do. What did you think of that advice? (Refer to Chapter 10.)

7. Do you think Ric's recommendation that you "graduate from college in four years, debt-free, on the dean's list, with a degree that lets you to have a career in the field you want to work in" is the right goal? (Refer to Chapter 5.)
   (a) Do you think each of these is achievable?
      (i) Graduating in four years
      (ii) Being debt-free
      (iii) Being on the dean's list (refer to Chapter 10)
      (iv) Getting a degree that lets you enter the career you want
   (b) If you're unsure about any of these or if you're concerned that any of them aren't realistically achievable, what do you think you should do?

   Adults, you're not trying to dissuade the student from college here; rather, your goal is for you all to formulate an action plan that will produce a good outcome for the student.

8. Were you surprised to learn the true cost of college? (Refer to Chapters 7 and 8.)
   (a) What do you think about how the cost rises every year?
   (b) What do you think about the impact of student loans?

9. Ric offered lots of ideas that can help you reduce the cost of getting a degree. Let's talk about each one and see if you feel that any of them are worth doing. (Refer to Chapter 9.)
   (a) Taking AP or DE classes in high school
   (b) Taking CLEP or DSST exams in high school
   (c) Attending community college for the first two years

- (d) Choosing a school that offers free degrees
- (e) Working full-time and attending college part-time, and choosing an employer that will pay for some or all of your tuition
- (f) Going to a school that's within a three-hour drive of home
- (g) Living at home while you attend college

10. Ric described the education benefits offered by ROTC and the U.S. military. Does the idea of enlisting appeal to you? (Refer to Chapter 9.)

11. Ric said lots of students go to college despite having no idea what career they want to pursue. He called that a mistake. Do you agree with him? Why or why not? (Refer to Chapter 10.)

12. Ric described the different kinds of employers that are out there. Did any appeal to you in particular? (Refer to Chapter 10.)

13. Ric also emphasized the idea of starting your own business. (Refer to Chapter 10.)
    - (a) Have you ever thought of doing that? Does the idea appeal to you?
        - (i) If so, what kind of business would you like to start? People embrace entrepreneurship or they don't, so adults mustn't push this one. But if a teen expresses an interest in this idea, then the adults and teen must devote lots of time and attention to learning about entrepreneurship and starting/operating a business. You all – and particularly the teen – should read lots of books, watch lots of videos and talk to lots of

business owners (both small family-owned shops and founders of medium- to large-sized companies).

14. Are you sure that the job you're thinking about requires that you get a college degree? (Refer to Chapter 10.)
15. What did you think of Ric's description of how he studied? (Refer to Chapter 10.)
    (a) Is that something you think you *need* to do?
    (b) Is it something you'd *like* to do?
    (c) Is it something you think you *can* do?
16. Have you thought about whether you'll need to go to graduate school? (Refer to Chapter 10.)
    (a) Do you think you might want to?
    (b) Do you think you might have to – and does that change how you're thinking or feeling about the career you've been envisioning?
    (c) Is grad school worth the cost, in terms of time, effort and money?

    Adults, don't be judgmental here; use this question as an opportunity for you all to explore the benefits versus the costs.
17. How much do we need to be thinking about AI and how it's going to change the field you're thinking of entering, or the availability of jobs in the field you want to pursue? (Refer to Chapter 10.)
    (a) What do you think we should do to try to figure this out?

    This is a great opportunity for adults and the teenager to design and embark on a learning journey together.

18. What do you think of Ric's idea that you consider an apprenticeship instead of college? (Refer to Chapter 10.)
19. Whaddya say we investigate together the financial health of the schools you're thinking of applying to? (Refer to Chapter 10.)

    This is another great opportunity for adults and the teen to design and embark on a learning journey together.
20. Have we talked with you about what we have or haven't done to pay for college?

    (a) **What questions do you have about paying for college?**
    College is one of the most important conversations adults must have with teenagers. As with those other adult topics, this is not the time for adults to refrain from telling teens the truth. They'll find out eventually, anyway – and the sooner they know the truth, the better.

Glossary

ABD all but dissertation; refers to people who have completed all the requirements to obtain their doctorate degree, except that their dissertation isn't finished

American Dream owning a home

Cum Laude a Latin phrase, conferred on students who graduate "with honors"

Dean's List a list of students who achieved the highest GPA each semester

Delinquency refers to borrowers who have not made payments in the past 90 days or more

Down Payment the cash you pay when buying real estate; the remainder of the purchase price is obtained by securing a loan

Food Insecurity not having access to food, or enough money to buy it

Garnishment seizure of your money by a court or government agency due to your failure to pay taxes, fines, penalties or the interest and principal on a loan

GPA grade point average; generally, 4.0 is equivalent to straight As

In-State refers to college students whose legal residence is in the same state as the school they are attending

Living Paycheck to Paycheck spending all of one's income on necessities, such as food, medicine and housing

Magna Cum Laude a Latin phrase, conferred on students who graduate "with high honors"

Mortgage the loan you obtain when borrowing money to buy real estate

Out-of-State refers to college students whose legal residence is not in the same state as the school they are attending

Pension a retirement program offered by some employers; employers who work full-time for a minimum number of years (typically 20 or more) are entitled to receive a monthly income for the remainder of their lifetime. The amount of income provided depends on a variety of factors, including the employee's salary history and number of years worked, and whether the employee wants payments to last for their lifetime, or both theirs and their spouse's lifetimes

Principal the amount you borrow when obtaining a loan

Private Sector businesses operating in commerce

Public Sector the government

Qualifying Credits college credits that apply to the college degree you are seeking to attain; not all classes qualify toward every degree

ROI return on investment; refers to your financial gain or loss

Separated from Service   when you lose your job because the employer has eliminated your position, not because of poor job performance

SME   subject-matter expert; one who is proficient in their field

Subsidies   money or services provided for free to an individual by a government agency

Summa Cum Laude   a Latin phrase, conferred on students who graduate "with highest honors"

Third Place   a social setting apart from home, work or school

Trade Association   a group of companies in the same industry that work together to resolve common issues

Undecided or Undeclared   a college student who has not chosen a major field of study

Winter Session   four-week college courses held during the December/New Year's break

Work-Life Balance   recognition that work and personal lives are equally important

Zero-Sum   situations that result in one person losing for each person who succeeds

Sources

Chapter 1

Credit Card Debt
https://www.lendingtree.com/credit-cards/study/credit-card-debt-statistics/

Mortgage Debt
https://www.lendingtree.com/home/mortgage/u-s-mortgage-market-statistics/

Automobile Debt
https://tradingeconomics.com/united-states/debt-balance-auto-loans

Jobs with Highest Work-Life Balance Satisfaction
https://www.theforage.com/blog/careers/jobs-with-highest-satisfaction

Average Salary of New College Graduates
https://www.naceweb.org/docs/default-source/default-document-library/2024/publication/executive-summary/2024-nace-winter-salary-survey-executive-summary.pdf?Status=Master&sfvrsn=b8ff91c4_3

SOURCES

Earnings of Bachelor's Degree Holders vs. Those with Only a High School Diploma
https://www.aplu.org/our-work/4-policy-and-advocacy/publicuvalues/employment-earnings/

Lifetime Earnings of Bachelor's Degree Holders vs. High School Graduates
https://www.ssa.gov/policy/docs/research-summaries/education-earnings.html

Job Opportunities for Bachelor's Degree Holders vs. High School Graduates
https://www.aplu.org/our-work/4-policy-and-advocacy/publicuvalues/employment-earnings/

Unemployment Rate for College Graduates vs. Those with Only a High School Diploma
https://www.pewresearch.org/short-reads/2022/04/12/10-facts-about-todays-college-graduates/

Average Time to Find a New Job After Layoff, College Graduates vs. High School Graduates
https://www.bls.gov/news.release/empsit.t12.htm

Likelihood of Job Layoff, College Graduates vs. Those with High School Diploma
https://www.intoo.com/us/blog/19-fascinating-stats-on-layoff-anxiety-infographic/#:~:text=Losing%20a%20job%20is%20not%20uncommon%2C%20but%20men%20are%20more,terminated%20three%20or%20more%20times

Amount of Credit Card Debt by Education
https://www.newyorkfed.org/microeconomics/hhdc

Cost of Health Insurance
https://www.kff.org/health-costs/

Cost of Child Care
https://www.care.com/c/how-much-does-child-care.cost/

Average 401(k) Employer Match
https://www.uschamber.com/co/run/human-resources/401k-company-match-plan#:~:text=According%20to%20Vanguard's%202024%20data%2C%20the%20average,covering%20up%20to%206.99%%20of%20employee%20contributions

Smoking by Education Level
https://www.cdc.gov/tobacco/campaign/tips/resources/data/cigarette-smoking-in-united-states.html

Health of College Graduates vs. People with Only a High School Diploma
https://odphp.health.gov/healthypeople/priority-areas/social-determinants-health/literature-summaries/enrollment-higher-education

Life Expectancy of People with a College Degree vs. People with Only a High School Diploma
https://www.economist.com/graphic-detail/2021/03/17/educated-americans-live-longer-as-others-die-younger

https://odphp.health.gov/healthypeople/priority-areas/social-determinants-health/literature-summaries/enrollment-higher-education

https://www.economist.com/graphic-detail/2021/03/17/educated-americans-live-longer-as-others-die-younger

SOURCES

Divorce Rates by Education Level
https://www.bls.gov/opub/mlr/2024/article/patterns-of-marriage-and-divorce-from-ages-15-to-55-evidence-from-the-nlsy79.htm

Money as a Cause of Divorce
https://www.cnbc.com/select/national-debt-relief-survey-debt-reason-for-divorce/

Likelihood of Attending College If a Parent Attended
https://www.pewresearch.org/social-trends/2021/05/18/first-generation-college-graduates-lag-behind-their-peers-on-key-economic-outcomes/

Strength of Family Relationships by Education
https://pmc.ncbi.nlm.nih.gov/articles/PMC9510327/

Children Outcomes by Education Level
https://pubmed.ncbi.nlm.nih.gov/35554528/

Place-Based Friendships by Education Level
https://www.americansurveycenter.org/research/the-college-connection-the-education-divide-in-american-social-and-community-life/

https://www.businessinsider.com/college-graduates-more-likely-have-friends-participate-community-civil-engagement-2024-10

Community Engagement by Education Level
https://www.americansurveycenter.org/research/the-college-connection-the-education-divide-in-american-social-and-community-life/

https://www.aplu.org/our-work/4-policy-and-advocacy/publicuvalues/societal-benefits/

Sources

Career and Financial Benefits of a College Degree
https://www.pewresearch.org/short-reads/2022/04/12/10-facts-about-todays-college-graduates/

Job Opportunities for College Graduates vs. Non-graduates
https://www.aplu.org/our-work/4-policy-and-advocacy/publicuvalues/employment-earnings/

Career Advancement Potential by Education Level
https://bachelors-completion.northeastern.edu/news/is-a-bachelors-degree-worth-it/

Critical Thinking and Problem-Solving Skills by Education Level
https://bachelors-completion.northeastern.edu/news/is-a-bachelors-degree-worth-it/

Networking Opportunities by Education Level
https://bachelors-completion.northeastern.edu/news/is-a-bachelors-degree-worth-it/

Personal Achievement by Education Level
https://bachelors-completion.northeastern.edu/news/is-a-bachelors-degree-worth-it/

Health and Well-Being by Education Level
https://allaccess.collegeboard.org/education-pays-2023-presents-data-benefits-education-individuals-and-society

Civic Engagement by Education Level
https://allaccess.collegeboard.org/education-pays-2023-presents-data-benefits-education-individuals-and-society

Access to Benefits by Education Level
https://allaccess.collegeboard.org/education-pays-2023-presents-data-benefits-education-individuals-and-society

SOURCES

Mortality Rates by Education Level
pmc.ncbi.nlm.nih.gov

Risk of Death by Education Level
https://www.healthdata.org/news-events/newsroom/news-releases/learning-life-higher-level-education-lower-risk-dying

Smoking Rates by Education Level
archpublichealth.biomedcentral.com

Physical Activity by Education Level
archpublichealth.biomedcentral.com

Access to Healthcare by Education Level
archpublichealth.biomedcentral.com

Stress of Being Laid Off
https://www.intoo.com/us/blog/19-fascinating-stats-on-layoff-anxiety-infographic/

https://www.pewresearch.org/social-trends/2021/05/18/first-generation-college-graduates-lag-behind-their-peers-on-key-economic-outcomes/

Economic Stability by Education Level
https://www.bls.gov/emp/tables/unemployment-earnings-education.htm

Health Outcomes by Education Level
https://www.pewresearch.org/social-trends/2021/05/18/first-generation-college-graduates-lag-behind-their-peers-on-key-economic-outcomes/

Social and Professional Networks by Education Level
https://www.pewresearch.org/social-trends/2021/05/18/first-generation-college-graduates-lag-behind-their-peers-on-key-economic-outcomes/

Chapter 2

Percent of College Students Who Drop Out

https://educationdata.org/college-dropout-rates#:~:text=Nationwide%20College%20Dropout%20Rates,States%20as%20of%20July%202020

Percent of College Graduates Who Chose the Wrong School or Major

https://stradaeducation.org/value/do-you-regret-your-college-choices/

https://www.newsnationnow.com/us-news/education/survey-these-are-the-top-college-majors-people-regret/

https://www.bestcolleges.com/news/almost-half-job-seeking-graduates-regret-their-major/

Percent of College Graduates who Regret Going to College

https://www.insidehighered.com/news/quick-takes/2024/10/11/report-quarter-grads-say-they-regret-going-college

Percent of College Graduates Underemployed

https://www.pewresearch.org/short-reads/2022/04/12/10-facts-about-todays-college-graduates/

https://www.resumebuilder.com/one-third-of-recent-college-grads-are-working-at-jobs-that-dont-require-a-college-education/

https://www.evidencebasedmentoring.org/half-of-college-graduates-have-jobs-that-dont-use-their-degrees/

https://stradaeducation.org/wp-content/uploads/2024/02/Talent-Disrupted.pdf

Percent of College Graduates Living with Parents

https://www.nahb.org/blog/2024/01/young-adults-living-at-home

SOURCES

https://newsroom.bankofamerica.com/content/dam/newsroom/docs/2024/BofA_BMH_GenZsurvey%202024%20Report.pdf

College Wealth Gap

https://www.stlouisfed.org/on-the-economy/2019/february/is-college-still-worth-it-complicated

College Dropout Rate

https://educationdata.org/college-dropout-rates#:~:text=Nationwide%20College%20Dropout%20Rates,States%20as%20of%20July%202020

https://educationdata.org/college-dropout-rates#:~:text=Between%20the%20fall%20semesters%20of,full%2Dtime%20freshmen%20dropped%20out

Depression Among College Students

https://www.acha.org/ncha/data-results/survey-results/academic-year-2023-2024/

Suicide Data Among College Students

https://www.studentloanplanner.com/mental-health-awareness-survey/

https://www.samhsa.gov/data/sites/default/files/report_3452/ShortReport-3452.html#:~:text=Results%3A%20About%209.5%20million%20adults,percent%20of%20the%20adult%20population

Chapter 3

Parent Concerns About College

https://www.insidehighered.com/news/students/financial-aid/2024/08/22/parents-value-clear-communication-about-college-cost-survey

Percent of Parents Recommending College
https://news.gallup.com/poll/344201/nearly-half-parents-noncollege-paths.aspx#:~:text=54%25%20of%20parents%20would%20prefer,would%20prefer%20another%20postsecondary%20option

Reasons High School Students Don't Go to College
https://www.bestcolleges.com/news/analysis/why-high-school-grads-are-saying-no-to-college/

Views of the Value of College
https://www.wsj.com/articles/americans-are-losing-faith-in-college-education-wsj-norc-poll-finds-3a836ce1

Percent Saying College Isn't Worth the Cost
https://www.pewresearch.org/social-trends/2024/05/23/is-college-worth-it-2/

Percent of College Graduates Saying They Would Do It Differently If They Could
https://www.bestcolleges.com/blog/college-graduate-majors-survey/

Percent Expressing Concern for College Costs
https://www.bestcolleges.com/news/analysis/why-high-school-grads-are-saying-no-to-college/
https://www.businessinsider.com/college-professor-parents-stop-forcing-kids-into-college-2024-5

Percent Saying Jobs Are Readily Available Without a College Degree
https://www.newsnationnow.com/us-news/education/high-school-grads-college/

Percent Expressing Skepticism About the Value of a College Degree
https://www.insidehighered.com/news/admissions/traditional-age/2024/06/03/reaching-those-who-start-college-applications-dont

SOURCES

Percent Saying College Is Bad for Mental Health
https://www.bestcolleges.com/news/analysis/why-high-school-grads-are-saying-no-to-college/

Percent Saying Children Are Not Prepared for College
https://www.businessinsider.com/college-professor-parents-stop-forcing-kids-into-college-2024-5

Percent Questioning the Value of a Degree
https://www.businessinsider.com/college-professor-parents-stop-forcing-kids-into-college-2024-5

Percent Choosing Alternative Career Opportunities
https://www.businessinsider.com/college-professor-parents-stop-forcing-kids-into-college-2024-5

Decline in College Enrollment
newsnationnow.com

Percent of High School Seniors Immediately Enrolling in College
nces.ed.gov

newsnationnow.com

Percent of High School Graduates Enrolled in College Immediately After Graduation, 2005
bls.gov

Percent of High School Graduates Enrolled in College Immediately After Graduation, 2016
nces.ed.gov

Percent of High School Graduates Enrolled in College Immediately After Graduation, 2023
educationdata.org

Undergraduate Enrollment
highereddive.com

Freshman Enrollment
highereddive.com

Chapter 4

Percent of College Freshmen Undecided About Major
https://central.edu/academics/majors/exploring/
Percent of College Students Who Change Majors
https://nces.ed.gov/pubs2018/2018434.pdf
https://studentresearchgroup.com/statistics-about-changing-college-majors/
Average Income of College Graduates
https://www.bls.gov/opub/ted/2024/median-weekly-earnings-of-full-time-workers-with-only-a-bachelors-degree-1541-in-q2-2024.htm
High Paying Jobs Not Requiring a College Degree
https://www.asvabprogram.com/media-center-article/194
Top Video Gamers
https://www.esportsearnings.com/players/highest-earnings-top-200
Peak Viewer of Gamer Tournaments
https://www.statista.com/statistics/507491/esports-tournaments-by-number-viewers-global/#:~:text=The%20League%20of%20Legends%202024,with%206.4%20million%20peak%20viewers

Chapter 5

Student Loans and Home Ownership
https://educationdata.org/student-loan-debt-homeownership#:~:text=Homeownership%20is%205.8%25%20higher%20among,them%20from%20buying%20a%20home

SOURCES

Homeownership Among College Graduates
https://educationdata.org/student-loan-debt-homeownership#:~:text=Homeownership%20is%205.8%25%20higher%20among,them%20from%20buying%20a%20home

Percent of College Students with Student Debt and Average Balance, 1985
https://files.eric.ed.gov/fulltext/ED288474.pdf

Percent of College Students with Student Debt and Average Balance, 2024
https://collegeaffordability.urban.org/covering-expenses/borrowing/#:~:text=Many%20students%20borrow%20to%20fund,by%20the%20time%20they%20graduate

Age of First-Time Home Buyers
https://www.nar.realtor/newsroom/first-time-home-buyers-shrink-to-historic-low-of-24-as-buyer-age-hits-record-high

Student Loan Debt
https://educationdata.org/student-loan-debt-statistics#:~:text=Report%20Highlights.,borrowers%20have%20federal%20loan%20debt

Delays in Life Events Due to College Debt
https://news.gallup.com/poll/643328/student-loan-borrowers-delayed-major-life-events.aspx

Delay in Marriage, Children and Buying a Home Due to Student Loans
https://www.getbenepass.com/blog/what-is-the-average-cost-of-benefits-per-employee-the-complete-guide

Chapter 6

Percent of Adults Who Own Stocks
https://www.visualcapitalist.com/american-stock-ownership-by-share-of-financial-assets/

Cost of Vacation
https://www.bankrate.com/banking/cost-of-vacation/

Cost of Automobile
https://www.kbb.com/car-news/average-new-car-price-tops-47000/#:~:text=The%20average%20price%20Americans%20paid,year%20of%20unprecedented%20price%20increases

Cost of Auto Insurance
https://www.bankrate.com/insurance/car/average-cost-of-car-insurance/

Cost of Gasoline
https://www.energy.gov/eere/vehicles/articles/fotw-1177-march-15-2021-preliminary-data-show-average-fuel-economy-new-light

Average Miles Driven
https://www.policygenius.com/auto-insurance/average-miles-driven-by-state/

Dealer Fees
https://www.creditkarma.com/auto/i/dealer-fees-buying-car

Auto Loan Terms
https://www.creditkarma.com/auto/i/car-loan-term

Cost of Parking
https://www.geekwire.com/2017/inrix-study-find-americans-waste-73-billion-per-year-looking-parking-spot/

SOURCES

Cost of Weddings
https://www.theknot.com/content/wedding-data-insights/real-weddings-study

Cost of Insurance
https://www.bankrate.com/insurance/life-insurance/cost-of-raising-a-child/

Cost of Buying a Home
https://www.bankrate.com/mortgages/costs-of-buying-a-home/

Percent of College Graduates in Poverty
Intelligent.com https://www.intelligent.com/1-in-7-college-grads-earn-less-than-the-poverty-threshold/

Unemployment Rates
https://www.newyorkfed.org/research/college-labor-market#--:explore:unemployment

Teacher Burnout
https://www.devlinpeck.com/content/teacher-burnout-statistics

Cost of Vacation
https://www.bankrate.com/banking/cost-of-vacation/

Average Price of New Car
https://www.cbtnews.com/study-found-new-car-prices-surged-to-record-highs-leaving-used-cars-as-the-affordable-choice/#:~:text=A%20recent%20study%20by%20Edmunds,trend%20in%20consumer%20purchasing%20behavior

Average Auto Sales Tax
https://www.policygenius.com/auto-insurance/auto-tax-rate-by-state/#:~:text=Car%20sales%20tax%20rates%20fall,car%20tax%20rate%20at%200.0%25

Sources

Average Auto Insurance Cost
https://www.bankrate.com/insurance/car/average-cost-of-car-insurance/

Annual Cost of Auto Ownership
https://www.aaa.com/autorepair/articles/average-annual-cost-of-new-vehicle-ownership

Cost of Children
https://www.fns.usda.gov/research/cnpp/expenditures-children-families

Inflation Rates
https://www.usinflationcalculator.com/inflation/current-inflation-rates/

Average Wedding Cost
https://www.visualcapitalist.com/mapped-average-wedding-costs-by-state/#:~:text=Our%20venue%20is%20only%20$500,%2C%20setup%20and%20cleanup%2C%20etc

Consumer Expenditure Survey
https://www.bls.gov/cex/tables/calendar-year/mean-item-share-average-standard-error.htm

Average Price of New vs. Used Auto
https://www.wsj.com/business/autos/why-there-is-no-relief-ahead-for-high-used-car-prices-8d7617be?mod=Searchresults_pos1&page=1

Average Home Price
https://www.fool.com/the-ascent/research/average-house-price-state/

SOURCES

Consumer Expenditures by Income and Education
https://www.bls.gov/cex/tables/calendar-year/mean-item-share-average-standard-error.htm
Head Start
https://en.wikipedia.org/wiki/Head_Start_(program)
Temporary Assistance for Needy Families (TANF)
dhs.dc.gov
Supplemental Nutrition Assistance Program (SNAP)
aspe.hhs.gov
Low-Income Home Energy Assistance Program (LIHEAP)
aspe.hhs.gov
Housing Choice Vouchers (Section 8 Housing)
aspe.hhs.gov
Earned Income Tax Credit (EITC)
aspe.hhs.gov
Child Tax Credit
nerdwallet.com
https://crsreports.congress.gov/product/pdf/R/R41873
https://www.pgpf.org/article/what-is-the-child-tax-credit/
Child and Dependent Care Tax Credit
irs.gov
American Opportunity Tax Credit (AOTC)
irs.gov
Tax Credits
https://www.irs.gov/newsroom/tax-credits-for-individuals-what-they-mean-and-how-they-can-help-refunds

Sources

Poverty Rates
https://www.statista.com/statistics/233162/us-poverty-rate-by-education/

Parents Providing Financial Support to Adult Children
https://www.savings.com/insights/financial-support-for-adult-children-study

Median Savings of Boomers
https://www.investopedia.com/articles/personal-finance/011216/average-retirement-savings-age-2016.asp#:~:text=In%20Your%202060s,-This%20can%20be&text=Baby%20Boomers%20have%20a%20median,of%20%24609%2C230%20saved%20for%20retirement

Student Credit Card Use
https://www.salliemae.com/content/dam/slm/writtencontent/Research/Majoring_in_Money.pdf

Average Credit Card Interest Rate
https://www.cbsnews.com/news/how-long-will-it-take-to-pay-off-10000-in-credit-card-debt/

Chapter 7

Credits of Transfer Students
https://www.gao.gov/products/gao-17-574
https://blog.workday.com/en-us/transfer-credits-supporting-student-mobility-higher-education.html#:~:text=Students%20lose%20approximately%2043%25%20of,to%20get%20a%20bachelor's%20degree

SOURCES

Tuition and Fees
https://www.in2013dollars.com/College-tuition-and-fees/price-inflation

Education Level of Postal Workers
https://www.zippia.com/postal-worker-jobs/education/

Increase in College Costs
https://www.in2013dollars.com/College-tuition-and-fees/price-inflation

Cost of College
https://educationdata.org/average-cost-of-college

Cost of College Per Credit Hour for Tuition and Fees
https://educationdata.org/cost-of-a-college-class-or-credit-hour

Salaries, Five Years After College Graduation
https://fortune.com/2024/03/25/earn-100000-5-years-after-graduating-study-engineering-new-york-federal-reserve/

Chapter 8

Credit Card Delinquency Rate
https://www.newyorkfed.org/newsevents/news/research/2025/20250213

Average Monthly Student Loan Payment
https://www.federalreserve.gov/publications/2019-economic-well-being-of-us-households-in-2018-student-loans-and-other-education-debt.htm

Average Number of Student Debtors Not Making Payments
https://www.federalreserve.gov/publications/2019-economic-well-being-of-us-households-in-2018-student-loans-and-other-education-debt.htm

Sources

Number of Adults Who Dropped Out Of College
https://nscresearchcenter.org/some-college-no-credential/

Percent of College Students Who Graduate in Six Years
https://nscresearchcenter.org/completing-college/

Cost Of College, 1965
https://nces.ed.gov/programs/digest/d13/tables/dt13_330.10.asp

Percent of High School Graduates Who Go to College
https://www.bls.gov/opub/ted/2024/61-4-percent-of-recent-high-school-graduates-enrolled-in-college-in-october-2023.htm#:~:text=Of%20the%203.1%20million%20people,in%20October%20of%20that%20year

Average Pay of College Graduates, 1967
https://www.naceweb.org/job-market/compensation/salary-trends-through-salary-survey-a-historical-perspective-on-starting-salaries-for-new-college-graduates/

Average Pay of College Graduates, 2024
https://www.naceweb.org/docs/default-source/default-document-library/2024/publication/executive-summary/2024-nace-winter-salary-survey-executive-summary.pdf?Status=Master&sfvrsn=b8ff91c4_3

Percent of College Students with Student Loans
https://educationdata.org/student-loan-debt-statistics

Average Student Loan Balance
https://educationdata.org/student-loan-debt-statistics

Life Goal Delays Due to Student Debt
https://www.luminafoundation.org/resource/cost-of-college/#:~:text=Seventy%2Done%20percent%20of%20currently,complete%20their%20degree%20or%20credential

SOURCES

Percent Who Would Choose a Different Major
https://www.bestcolleges.com/blog/college-graduate-majors-survey/
How Students Spend Their Loans
https://www.usatoday.com/story/money/personalfinance/2016/10/18/student-loans-spend-drugs-alcohol/91915580/
Percent of College Freshmen Who Drop Out
https://educationdata.org/college-dropout-rates#:~:text=Between%20the%20fall%20semesters%20of,full%2Dtime%20freshmen%20dropped%20out
Percent of College Students Who Graduate After Six Years
https://nces.ed.gov/fastfacts/display.asp?id=40
College Graduation Rate
https://www.bestcolleges.com/research/college-graduation-rates/
https://www.highereddive.com/news/college-students-average-less-than-22-credits-in-their-first-year-too-few/628697/
Percent of Student Loans Cosigned
https://money.com/should-i-cosign-private-student-loan/#:~:text=Still%2C%20these%20private%20loans%20may,case%20is%20the%20college%20student
Amount of Student Loans Owed by Parents
https://www.bestcolleges.com/research/parent-plus-loans-statistics/
Scholarship Data
https://educationdata.org/scholarship-statistics
Amount of Student Loans Owed by Those Age 50+
https://www.aarp.org/money/personal-finance/student-debt-crisis-for-older-americans/
https://www.nclc.org/3-5-million-older-americans-have-over-125-billion-in-student-loans/

Sources

Social Security Benefits Garnished Due to Student Loans
https://www.studentloanplanner.com/social-security-garnished-student-loans/

How Long Student Debt Lasts
https://educationdata.org/average-student-loan-debt

Those Ages 60+ with Student Debt
https://www.nclc.org/wp-content/uploads/2024/09/Impact-of-Student-Debt-on-Older-Adults.pdf

Average Monthly Payment on Student Loans
https://thecollegeinvestor.com/33643/average-student-loan-monthly-payment/

Impact of Big Beautiful Tax Bill on Student Loan Repayments
Opinion | The Ugliness of the 'Big, Beautiful' Bill, in Charts - The New York Times

Student Loan Garnishment
https://www.ed.gov/about/news/press-release/us-department-of-education-begin-federal-student-loan-collections-other-actions-help-borrowers-get-back-repayment

Chapter 9

Percent of College Students Who Transfer
https://www.insidehighered.com/quicktakes/2015/07/08/more-third-college-students-transfer

Number of States with Free Community College
https://www.bestcolleges.com/news/analysis/2022/05/24/is-community-college-free/

SOURCES

Portion of Students Attending Community College
https://www.ed.gov/higher-education/find-college-or-educational-program/community-college/facts-at-a-glance

Number of States Offering Free Four-Year College Degrees
https://www.bankrate.com/loans/student-loans/states-with-free-college-tuition/#states-with

Free Colleges
https://www.nytimes.com/article/which-colleges-offer-free-tuition.html?smid=nytcore-ios-share&referringSource=articleShare

Chapter 10

Students Ages 30+
https://educationdata.org/college-enrollment-statistics#:~:text=9.19%25%20of%20all%20enrolled%20students,aged%2040%2D49%20years%20old

Number of Private-Sector Workers
https://data.bls.gov/timeseries/CES0500000001

Number of Public-Sector Workers
https://www.census.gov/library/publications/2024/econ/g24-aspep.html

Number of Federal Government Workers
https://www.pewresearch.org/short-reads/2025/01/07/what-the-data-says-about-federal-workers/

Salary of Mail Carriers
https://www1.salary.com/Salaries-for-u-s-postal-service-usps-mail-sorter-with-a-Bachelors-Degree
https://datausa.io/profile/soc/postal-service-mail-carriers#education

Top Jobs in State and Local Governments
https://www.bls.gov/spotlight/2021/occupational-employment-and-wages-in-state-and-local-government/#:~:text=The%20largest%20occupations%20in%20local,police%20and%20sheriff's%20patrol%20officers

Number of Self-Employed People
https://www.bls.gov/news.release/archives/empsit_04052024.htm

Walmart Manager Salaries
https://www.nbcnews.com/business/business-news/walmart-managers-can-earn-400000-year-no-college-stock-grant-rcna136364

Number of Walmart Stores in the United States
https://www.scrapehero.com/location-reports/Walmart-USA/

Number of Walmart Employees
https://www.inc.com/bill-murphy-jr/walmart-is-biggest-us-employer-heres-1-thing-employees-should-never-do.html

Number of Students Majoring in Sociology
https://www.collegefactual.com/majors/social-sciences/sociology/#:~:text=Sociology%20was%20the%2025th%20most,overall%20colleges%20for%20sociology%20students

Number of People Working as Sociologists
https://www.bls.gov/ooh/life-physical-and-social-science/sociologists.htm#:~:text=Sociologists%20also%20may%20specialize%20in,internships%20or%20by%20preparing%20reports

Percent of College Students Who Want to Work for Google
https://www.axios.com/2023/04/04/gen-z-jobs-employers-google-tesla-patagonia

SOURCES

College Graduates' Salaries vs. Expectation
https://www.bankrate.com/loans/student-loans/do-college-students-have-realistic-salary-expectations/

Percent of Workers with Degrees in Fields That Don't Require One
https://www.bls.gov/emp/tables/educational-attainment.htm

Items Pertaining to Item 5 Linebar
https://www.aplu.org/our-work/4-policy-and-advocacy/publicuvalues/employment-earnings/

https://www.forbes.com/sites/michaeltnietzel/2021/10/11/new-study-college-degree-carries-big-earnings-premium-but-other-factors-matter-too/

https://www.aplu.org/our-work/4-policy-and-advocacy/publicuvalues/employment-earnings

https://www3.weforum.org/docs/WEF_Future_of_Jobs_2020.pdf

https://www.whatjobs.com/news/stem-job-market-2025/

https://cew.georgetown.edu/cew-reports/the-college-payoff/

https://www.naceweb.org/talent-acquisition/candidate-selection/what-are-employers-looking-for-when-reviewing-college-students-resumes

https://www.parchment.com/blog/podcast-episode-35-naces-2025-job-outlook-for-graduates/

https://www.imf.org/en/Publications/fandd/issues/2020/12/WEF-future-of-jobs-report-2020-zahidi

https://www.skillreporter.com/editorial/world-economic-forum-future-of-jobs-2025-core-skills-of-2030/

https://www.weforum.org/agenda/2016/01/the-10-skills-you-need-to-thrive-in-the-fourth-industrial-revolution/http://dx.doi.org/10.6007/IJARBSS/v13-i11/19418

https://www.univariety.com/blog/corporate-leaders-with-humanities-degree/

https://collegecliffs.com/governors-degrees-earned/

https://www.washingtonpost.com/news/answer-sheet/wp/2017/12/20/the-surprising-thing-google-learned-about-its-employees-and-what-it-means-for-todays-students/

https://www.nytimes.com/2019/09/20/business/liberal-arts-stem-salaries.html

https://www.fastcompany.com/91328317/lets-stop-calling-them-soft-skills-theyre-the-hardest-

https://hrmpractice.com/the-origin-of-soft-skills/

https://www.library.hbs.edu/working-knowledge/why-soft-skills-still-matter-in-the-age-of-ai

https://www.forbes.com/sites/roncarucci/2024/02/06/in-the-age-of-ai-critical-thinking-is-more-needed-than-ever/

https://www.allaboutai.com/resources/critical-thinking-in-the-age-of-ai/

https://www.weforum.org/stories/2025/01/ai-workplace-skills/

Economic Order

https://www.weforum.org/stories/2025/01/ai-workplace-skills/

Using Pen and Paper for Recall

https://mindmatters.ai/2021/03/researchers-we-learn-better-using-paper-than-laptops-and-phones/

Average Cost of Law School

https://educationdata.org/average-cost-of-law-school

Average Cost of Medical School

https://educationdata.org/average-cost-of-medical-school

SOURCES

Average MBA Cost
https://www.mbaandbeyond.com/blog/mba-fees-in-the-usa#:~:text=On%20average%2C%20aspiring%20MBA%20candidates,to%20%24100%2C000%20per%20academic%20year

Percent of College Students in Graduate School
https://educationdata.org/college-enrollment-statistics#:~:text=17.13%25%20of%20all%20postsecondary%20students,a%20483%25%20increase%20from%201976

Amount of Student Debt – Graduate vs. Undergraduate Degree
https://educationdata.org/student-loan-debt-statistics#:~:text=Student%20Loan%20Borrower%20Statistics&text=20%25%20of%20all%20American%20adults,debt%20growth%20rate%20is%202.1%25

Number of Teachers with Graduate Degrees
https://www.nu.edu/blog/education-statistics/#:~:text=48%25%20of%20people%20employed%20in%20education%20have%20an%20advanced%20degree.&text=Between%202010%20and%202019%2C%20the,3.1%20million%20to%203.2%20million

Average Cost of Graduate Degree in Education
https://www.coursera.org/articles/masters-in-education

Cost of Online Graduate Degree in Education
https://www.geteducated.com/online-college-ratings-and-rankings/best-buy-lists/best-buy-online-masters-of-education/#/

Percent Who Say College Does Not Prepare Students for Jobs
https://www.highereddive.com/news/experience-prepared-workers-for-jobs/699746/

Percent of Bosses Who Say College Does Not Prepare Students for Jobs
https://www.cbsnews.com/miami/news/survey-4-in-10-business-leaders-say-recent-college-grads-not-ready-for-workforce/

Sources

Percents of Students Who Go to Out-of-State School
https://ticas.org/wp-content/uploads/2023/11/Hillman-Geography-of-Opportunity-Brief-1_2023.pdf

Tenure of College Presidents
https://www.acenet.edu/Documents/American-College-President-IX-2023.pdf

AT&T CEO on Need to Learn
https://www.nytimes.com/2016/02/14/technology/gearing-up-for-the-cloud-att-tells-its-workers-adapt-or-else.html#:~:text=invented%20the%20telephone.-,%E2%80%9CThere%20is%20a%20need%20to%20retool%20yourself%2C%20and%20you%20should,obsolete%20themselves%20with%20the%20technology.%E2%80%9D

NASA Head on Need to Learn
https://futurism.com/2-by-the-time-you-are-a-junior-in-college-what-you-learned-as-a-freshman-is-already-obsolete-nasa

Salary of Graphic Designers
https://www.bls.gov/ooh/arts-and-design/graphic-designers.htm

CPA Pass Rate
https://www.franklin.edu/blog/accounting-mvp/how-hard-is-the-cpa-exam#:~:text=About%20half%20of%20the%20individuals,highest%20pass%20rate%20at%2061.94%25

Average CPA Salary
https://accounting.uworld.com/cpa-review/cpa-career/cpa-salary/

Obsolete Jobs
https://en.wikipedia.org/wiki/List_of_obsolete_occupations

Highest and Lowest Paid Jobs 15 Years After Graduating
https://www.cnbc.com/2022/03/02/best-and-worst-paying-college-majors-for-graduates-aged-35-to-45.html

SOURCES

Handwriting vs. Typing
https://www.nbcnews.com/health/health-news/writing-by-hand-may-increase-brain-connectivity-rcna135880

Using AI to Write Papers
Opinion | How A.I. Could Make Us Dumber - The New York Times

Faculty Use of AI
https://www.nytimes.com/2025/05/14/technology/chatgpt-college-professors.html

Aneesh Raman, CEOO of LinkedIn, on Job Opportunities for College Grads
https://www.nytimes.com/2025/05/19/opinion/linkedin-ai-entry-level-jobs.html

Unemployment Rate for College Graduates
https://www.cbsnews.com/news/college-graduate-unemployed-technology-artificial-intelligence/

Potential Job Losses Due to Automation
https://www.gspublishing.com/content/research/en/reports/2023/03/27/d64e052b-0f6e-45d7-967b-d7be35fabd16.html

Percent of Workers Worried That Their Job Will Be Replaced by Technology
https://www.pwc.com/gx/en/issues/workforce/hopes-and-fears.html#:~:text=Red%20flag%20alert:%20the%20risk,a%20very%20large%20extent'%20responses)

Occupation That Will Have the Largest Net Job Growth
https://www.weforum.org/stories/2023/04/future-jobs-2023-fastest-growing-decline/#:~:text=What%20goes%20up%20%E2%80%A6,of%20Jobs%202023%20report%20notes

CEOs Warning of AI-Induced Job Losses
https://www.wsj.com/lifestyle/careers/ai-entry-level-jobs-graduates-b224d624?mod=Searchresults_pos1&page=1

Amazon CEO Email to Employees About AI
https://www.wsj.com/tech/ai/amazon-andy-jassy-ai-f34676e7

College Spending Budgets
https://www.wsj.com/articles/state-university-tuition-increase-spending-41a58100

Colleges at Risk of Closing
https://www.ey.com/en_us/insights/education/strategy-consulting-higher-ed-financial-risk-as-funds-expire

High-Paying Jobs That Don't Require a College Degree
https://www.asvabprogram.com/media-center-article/194

In-State vs. Out-of-State Tuition Cost
https://www.bestcolleges.com/resources/in-state-vs-out-of-state-tuition/

Age of College Students
https://educationdata.org/college-enrollment-statistics

Graduate Degrees That Fail to Lead to High Incomes
https://fortune.com/2024/11/28/masters-degrees-with-starting-salary-over-100k-students-worse-off-financially-after-program/

Acknowledgments

This book began as a two-day presentation I made to a group of high school students in New Jersey. I'd had numerous conversations with Rowan University President Ali A. Houshmand, PhD, and Sanford Tweedie, PhD, then dean of what was then called the Ric Edelman College of Communication & Creative Arts, and we'd shared our concerns that too many high school students were making bad decisions about college – choosing not to attend, or attending but selecting the wrong major or the wrong school, or incurring too much debt along the way. Worst of all, we agreed, far too many students leave college without attaining a degree. Clearly, the higher ed model is broken, and until it's fixed – until college is affordable and the graduation rate improved – we need to arm high school students with the information they need, so they can make an informed decision about college. So, with Ali's support and Sandy's guidance, we created this event. I'm grateful to them both. Many thanks also to Anthony Lowman, PhD, Rowan University chancellor; to Nawal Ammar, PhD, new dean of the Ric Edelman College of Communication, Humanities & Social Sciences; and especially to

ACKNOWLEDGMENTS

Brittany Petrella, associate vice president of University Advancement, who has the unfortunate job of serving as my university liaison. She's unflappable, highly professional, and always smiling – a real asset to both the university and me.

The student event we held was so successful – 90% of the participating students later said they'd changed their minds about which college to attend, and all responded that they now understand the importance of getting their degree in just four years (not six) – that I decided to convert my presentation into a book so we could get the content to every family that's struggling with the college decision. That's why I'm indebted to the folks at John Wiley & Sons. I have never enjoyed a better publishing experience, despite the crazy short production schedule (my fault, sorry). Many thanks to Publisher Shannon Vargo, who's a textbook (sorry) example of how a great publisher performs. My editor, Kevin Harreld, and managing editor, Susan Cerra, guided the project smoothly and efficiently, and made every interaction pleasant. Kudos and thanks to copyeditor Kim Wimpsett, who fixed all the grammatical inconsistencies and nonsensical sentences and to editorial assistant Delainey Henson, who was the person behind the scenes who really made things happen. This book was also improved with the help of Suganya Selvaraj, Wiley's content refinement specialist who managed the page proof and index reviews. And no matter how good something is, no one ever knows about it unless someone starts talking about it – so I'm very appreciative of the work done by marketing manager Jean-Karl Martin and his team. Leadership starts at the top, though, so I offer my thanks to Wiley CEO Matt Kissner, who gave the immediate go-ahead that made this all happen. Thank you, Matt, for your faith in me.

Acknowledgments

I also want to thank the members of my team who read the manuscript and offered insightful comments that materially improved the final version that you've read. The fingerprints of Maribeth Bluyus, Michaele Kayes, Nicole Ricciardi, Liz Dougherty and Rene Chaze can be found on virtually every page. Also thank you to MB's daughter, Emily, a sophomore and the only student who reviewed and commented on the manuscript. She offered comments that all the adults missed!

A shout-out to Skip and Joanie's adult daughter Mary, who begged me to include her name in these pages. I agreed for 10 bucks. But I didn't tell her that including her last name would be 20 bucks.

Finally and most importantly, thank you to my wife Jean. She's suffered through all of my book projects, tolerating my sequestering as I pound the keyboard for months. Jean has the patience of a saint, a trait instilled in her by her mom, Rita. I'm lucky both are in my life.

INDEX

Page numbers followed by *t* refer to tables.

A
AAA, 43
Accounting, 103, 137–138
Accreditation, 161
Active-duty personnel, 86
Admissions test(s), 79
Adult children, 51*t*
Advanced Placement (AP) classes, 78–81, 80*t*
Agricultural Age, 136
AI, 118–119, 128, 139–141
Alcoholic beverages, 48*t*
Amazon, 141
American College Health Associations, 18
American Council of Education, 168
"The American Dream," 43
American Educational Research Association, 40
American Foundation of Suicide Prevention, 19
American Red Cross, 98
American Survey Center, 11–12
Amodei, Dario, 140
Apartment List, 37
AP (Advanced Placement) classes, 78–81, 80*t*
Apprenticeship.gov, 152
Apprenticeships, 150–152
Aspen Economic Strategy Group, 37
Aspirations, 182
Assistance, government, 46, 49, 182–183
Associate's degrees, 83

INDEX

Association of Public an Land-Grant Universities, 12
AT&T, 178
Attendance, part-time, 85–89
Auditing, 96
Auditors, 138
Axios/Generation Lab, 121

B

Baby Boomers, 50
Bankrate, 41
Benefits, employee, 6–7, 102–103
Benefits, of college, 1–13
   community engagement, 12
   employee benefits, 6–7
   health, 9–10
   relationships, 10–12
   salary, 2–6
   work-life balance, 7–8
Best Colleges, 66
Big Beautiful Tax Bill Act, 72–73
Birmingham Southern College, 160
Bloomberg, Michael, 166
Bond issuers, 161–162
Books and supplies, 57
Boston University, 158
Branding, for entrepreneurs, 104
Bureau of Labor Statistics, 2, 8, 10, 57, 97, 109, 121, 136–137
Burning Glass Institute, 16, 140

Business expenses, 102
Business management, 104

C

Campus visits, 169–170
Car(s), 51t
Carnegie, 22
Cash contributions, 48t
Cellular phone service, 48t, 51t
Center for Professional Success, 130
Center for the Advancement of Women in Communication Writing Center, 130
Centers for Disease Control, 9
Central College, 27
Charities, 98
Chief academic officer, 168
Chief development officer, 168
Child care, 6
Children, supporting your adult, 51t
Child Tax Credit, 49
CLEP (College-Level Examination Program), 81–82
Closures, school, 156–160
Clothing, 48t
College, deciding to go to, 25–33
College admissions tests, 79
College Board, 79, 81

Index

College credits, 55, 56, 56t, 78–81
College Factual, 121
College-Level Examination Program (CLEP), 81–82
College presidents, 167–169
Columbia University, 160
Community college, 82–83
Community engagement, 12
Commute, 89–90
Compliance, 103
Construction on campus, 169
Contributions, cash, 48t
Conversation starters, 181–188
Cost(s):
    of AP and DE classes, 80t
    general college, 55–59
    lifestyle, 42–52
    living, 42–46
    minimizing, 77–93, *see* Minimizing costs
    out-of-state and private school, 59–61
    and spending, 46–52
    of U.S. households, 45t
Coursera, 107
Credibility, 107
Credit cards, 4–5, 51t, 69–70
Cruise, Tom, 45
Customer service, 104

D

DANTES Subject Standardized Tests (DSST), 81–82
Data, enrollment, 164–165
DEA, 88
Dean's list, 37, 112, 168
Debt, graduating without, 36–37
DE (Dual Enrollment) classes, 78–81, 80t
Delayed graduation, 58–59
Delta, 151
Deming, David, 124
Department chair, 168
Department head, 168
Department of Education, 82
Department of Labor, 151
Depression, 18
Director of academic advising, 168
Director of admissions, 168
Director of alumni relations, 168
Director of career services, 168
Discretionary spending, 51t
Down payments, 43
Drexel University, 158
Drones, 137
Dropping out, 71, 95–96
DSST (DANTES Subject Standardized Tests), 81–82
Dual Enrollment (DE) classes, 78–81, 80t

E

EAB, 22
Earned income, 4
Earned Income Tax Credit, 49
Earning potential, 101
EDI, *see* Education Data Initiative
Edmunds, 42
Education budgets, 158
Education Data Initiative (EDI), 37, 56, 65, 71, 96
Employee benefits, 6–7, 102–103
Employer, considering your future, 97–109
Endowment funds, 166–167
Engagement, community, 12
Enrollment data, 164–165
Entertainment, 47*t*
Entrepreneurship, 100–109
   benefits of, 100–102
   with college degree, 106–107
   downsides of, 102–106
   without college degree, 107–109
Esports, 29
Expenses, *see* Cost(s)
Extinct jobs, 141–142, 143*t*–146*t*
E&Y, 160, 164

F

FAFSA, 84
Farley, Jim, 140
Federal Reserve Bank of New York, 4, 124
Federal Reserve Bank of St. Louis, 16, 43
Fees, underwriting, 162
Fiverr, 140
Flexibility, 100
Food:
   costs of, 47*t*
   food stamps, 49
   insecurity of, 71
Forage, 8
Ford, 140
Foreclosures, 68
For-profit companies, 97
Foundation for Research on Equal Opportunity, 134, 171
4.0 GPA, 114–118
Freedom, 100
Fry Scholarship, 87
Funds, endowment, 166–167
Further education requirements, 132–133
Future career, major mismatch with, 16
Future of Jobs report (World Economic Forum), 127

G

Gallup, 15, 21
Garnishing wages, 72

Gates Foundation, 22
General Accountability Office, 58
Gettysburg College, 158
GI Bill, 87
Goal-setting, 35–38
Goldman Sachs, 140
Google, 137, 151
Government Accountability Office, 159
Government assistance, 46, 49, 182–183
Grade point average (GPA), 114–118
Grades, 55, 112–119
Graduation, delayed, 58–59
Groceries, 51*t*

H
Harber, Alan, 160
Harm, self, 18–19
Harris Poll, 3
Harvard, 160
Head Start, 49
Health:
    college affecting, 9–10
    institution, 161–170
    mental, 18–19
Healthcare, 47*t*, 51*t*
Health insurance, 6
Hechinger Report, 160
Hermes, 151–152

High Point University, 158
Housing, costs of, 47*t*
Housing Choice Vouchers, 49
Humanities, 128

I
IBM, 141, 151
Income:
    and American spending, 47*t*–48*t*
    earned, 4
    instability in, with entrepreneurship, 102
    of U.S. households, 45*t*
Indiana University of Pennsylvania, 158
Industrial Age, 136
Information Age, 136
In-state colleges, 56
Institute of Electrical and Electronics Engineers, 128
Institution health, 161–170
Insurance, 6, 48*t*
Interest, 162
Internal Revenue Service, 4
Investopedia, 50

J
Jassy, Andy, 141
Job(s):
    extinct, 141–142, 143*t*–146*t*
    high-paying, 28*t*

Job(s) (*Continued*)
  impact of chosen job, 153–154
  lack of prospects for, 120–131
  safe long term, 147*t*–150*t*
  without a degree, 110*t*, 111*t*
  "zero-sum," 122
Job Outlook (National Association of Colleges and Employers), 127
Johns Hopkins University, 165
JPMorgan Chase, 140

K
Kaufman, Micha, 140
Key performance indicators (KPIs), 162–163
The Knot, 43
Krishna, Arvind, 141

L
Lake, Marianne, 140
Law school, 132–133
Learning, lifelong, 177–179
Lenders, 67–70
Lending Tree, 37
Levin, Jon, 160
Liberal arts majors, 129
Life insurance, 48*t*
Lifelong learning, 177–179
Lifestyle, 39–53
  about, 39–41
  considering, 153–156

  costs and spending, 42–52
  taxes, 41–42
Lightfoot, Robert M., Jr., 178
LinkedIn, 139
Living at home, 90–91
Loans:
  mortgages, 43, 51*t*, 67–69
  Parent PLUS Loans, 73
  student, *see* Student loans
Low grades, 112–119
Low-Income Home Energy Assistance Program, 49
Low-income households, 51–52, 84
Lumina Foundation, 66
Lütke, Tobi, 141
LVMH, 151–152

M
Major(s):
  changing your, 58
  choosing your, 63–65
  and future career goals, 16
  liberal arts, 129
  undecided, 27
Marketing, 104
Marriage, 10–11
Master's degree in education (M.Ed), 134–135
Maturity date, 162
McKinsey, 40

M.Ed (master's degree in education), 134–135
Mental health, 18–19
Messi, Lionel, 45
Milliken, James, 160
Minimizing costs:
   Advanced Placement classes, 78–81
   college credit, 78–81
   College-Level Examination Program, 81–82
   community college, 82–83
   DANTES Subject Standardized Tests, 81–82
   by living at home, 90–91
   online courses, 92
   part-time attendance, 85–89
   with a short commute, 89–90
   tuition-free colleges, 83–84
Mistakes, 95–176
   apprenticeships, 150–152
   employer considerations, 97–109
   further education requirements, 132–133
   lack of job prospects, 120–131
   lifestyle considerations, 153–156
   low grades, 112–119
   ROI, 133–135
   rushing into college, 95–96
   school closures, 156–170
   technology influences, 136–150
   trust in colleges/universities, 170–174
   unnecessary degrees, 109–111
MIT, 84, 118
Money magazine, 73
Mortgages, 43, 51*t*, 67–69
MyCAA, 88
MyPerfectResume, 8

N

NASA, 129, 178
National Alliance on Mental Illness, 18
National Association of Colleges and Employers, 127
National Association of Home Builders, 91
National Association of Realtors, 37
National Center for Education Statistics, 22, 64, 73
National Consumer Law Center, 74
National Education Association, 134
National Football League (NFL), 122–123
National Institutes of Health, 11
National Student Clearinghouse Research Center, 17, 57, 58
National University, 134
Negotiations, 104

Networking, 106
New America, 74
Newbury College, 164
New York Federal Reserve, 63, 72
NFL (National Football League), 122–123
Non-profit organizations, 98
Northeastern University, 12

O
Online courses, 92
Out-of-state schools, 59–61, 172
Oxford Economics, 140
Oxford University, 137, 142, 147

P
Paid child care, 6
Paid health insurance, 6
Paid sick leave, 6
Paid vacation, 6
Parenthood, 11, 51*t*
Parent PLUS Loans, 73
Part-time attendance, 85–89
Part-time work, 85
Passions, 65, 101, 105
Payments, down, 43
Payscale, 8
Pell Grants, 83, 84
Penn State, 159
Pensions, 47*t*

Perils, of college, 15–20
   attending vs. graduating, 17
   future career and major mismatch, 16
   mental health and trauma, 18–19
   student loans, 16–17
Personal care, 48*t*
Peter G. Peterson Foundation, 37
Pew Research Center, 2, 16
Potential, earning, 101
Private schools, 59–61, 60*t*
Private sector, 97–98
Productivity, 98–99
Provost, 168
Public in-state schools, 60*t*
Public out-of-state schools, 60*t*
Public sector, 97, 99

R
Raman, Aneesh, 139
Real Estate Witch, 121
Reinhart, James, 141
Relationships, 10–12
Remote work, 154
Rent, 51*t*
Reserve Officers' Training Corps (ROTC), 88–89
Resilience, 104–105
Retirement savings, 6–7, 101

Return on investment (ROI), 64, 133–135
Risk, and debt, 69–70
ROI (return on investment), 64, 133–135
ROTC (Reserve Officers' Training Corps), 88–89
Rowan University, 29, 123, 129–131
Rowling, JK, 45
Ruination, 65
Rutgers University, 157

S
Safe long term jobs, 147*t*–150*t*
Salary.com, 109
Salaries, 2–6
   10 year after graduation, 126*t*
   in private sector, 98
   in public sector, 99
SAT college admissions test, 79
Savings, retirement, 6–7, 101
Savings.com, 50
Schools:
   in-state, 56
   law, 132–133
   out-of-state, 59–61, 172
   private, 59–61, 60*t*
   public in-state, 60*t*
   public out-of-state, 60*t*
School closures, 156–170

Science, technology, engineering, and math (STEM), 123–125
Section 8 housing, 49
Self-employment, 100–101
Self harm, 18–19
Self-motivation, 104–105
Semesters, 56
Shipman, Claire, 160
Shopify, 141
SHRM (Society for Human Resource Management), 151
Sick leave, 6
Social security, 47*t*
Social Security Administration, 2
Societal views, of college, 21–23
Society for Human Resource Management (SHRM), 151
Sociologists, 121
Spending, 46–52, 47*t*–48*t*, 51*t*.
   See also Costs
Stamps, food, 49
Stanford University, 160
STEM (science, technology, engineering, and math), 123–125
Stephenson, Randall, 178
Strada Education Foundation, 15, 16
Stress, 10
Student Borrower Protection Center, 73

Student Loan Planner, 18–19
Student loans:
    parental help with, 51*t*
    risks of, 16–17, 65–66
    understanding, 67–74
Study.com, 118
Study Hall, 81
Success, defining, 26
Suicide, 18–19
Supplemental Nutrition
    Assistance Program, 49
Supplies, 57
Swift, Taylor, 45

T
Tax(es), 41–42
    benefits, for entrepreneurships, 101
    refunds, 49
    tax credits, 49
Technology, 104, 136–150
Temporary Assistance for Needy Families, 46
Texas Tech, 158
The Conference Board, 8
ThredUp, 141
3+3 Law Program, 130
Time management, 104, 107
Tobacco, 48*t*, 52
Trade association, 152

Trading Economics, 37
Transferring schools, 159–160, 173
Transportation, 47*t*
Transunion, 72
Trauma, 18–19
Travel, 155
Trump, Donald, 51, 72–73, 160
Trust, 170–174
The Truth About Your Future (Edelman), 136, 158
Tuition:
    discounts on, 165–166
    parental help with, 51*t*
    publish rates of, 174
Tuition-free colleges, 83–84
Tuition reimbursement
    programs, 86
Turnover, 168–169

U
UCLA (University of California Los Angeles), 160
Udemy, 107
Undecided major, 27
Underwriting fee, 162
Unemployment, 2–3
University of Alabama, 158
University of California
    Los Angeles (UCLA), 160

University of Florida, 159
University of Kentucky, 157
University of Maryland, 83
University of Memphis, 158
University of Minnesota, 157
University of Nebraska, 157
University of Oklahoma, 157–158
University of Washington, 10
Unnecessary degrees, 109–111
U.S. Armed Forces, 86–89
U.S. Department of Agriculture, 44
U.S. Department of Education, 18, 163
U.S. Department of Health and Human Services, 10
U.S. News, 8
USA Today, 15
USPS, 109
Utilities, 47t

V

Vacations, 6, 51t
VA Work-Study Program, 87
Veterans, 87
VetSuccess on Campus, 87

Video gamers, 29
Visits, campus, 169–170
Vocational Rehabilitation & Employment program, 87

W

Wages, garnishing, 72
Wall Street Journal, 157–159
Walmart, 120
Wealth, salaries and, 3–6
Welfare, 46, 49
West Virginia University, 159
Work:
  part-time, 85
  remote, 154
Work-life balance, 7–8, 100, 105
World Economic Forum, 127, 140

Y

Yellow Ribbon Program, 87
YouTube, 107

Z

"Zero-sum" jobs, 122
Zuckerberg, Mark, 45